SURVIVING THE COMING COFFEE CRISIS

By Adam Michaels

ISBN: 978-1-62409-024-0

TABLE OF CONTENTS

Coffee Crisis Introduction – Trouble Brewing?

"By failing to prepare, you are preparing to fail."
-Benjamin Franklin.

The world today is nearing a tipping point on a number of levels. The financial crisis continues to topple governments and spark massive uprisings. The massive droughts plague the world's breadbaskets, and a rapidly growing global population; the challenges facing what we call "civilization" are growing every day. As these problems continue to compound one another, authorities on every continent are losing control of the situation.

In fact, the more time you spend investigating, the more you realize how these problems are interrelated. Global financial collapses, resource shortages, and civil unrest are all warning signs that the world in which we live is becoming less stable. Right now, millions of Americans just like you are taking notice and beginning to ask themselves some very tough questions about emergency preparedness.

Do you have what you need to survive a crisis? Have you created a plan that protects your family in the event of a monetary collapse, a major terrorist attack, or even a constitutional crisis? You're probably asking yourself, "Why am I talking about terrorism and global finance in a book about coffee?"

I promise, by the end of this introduction, you'll understand just how a commodity like coffee can become a lens through which you can see trouble brewing around the world. Suffice to say, coffee has planted itself firmly at the center of American life. The majority of American households brew coffee each morning. Many are loyal Starbucks customers. Others make their living growing, trading, transporting, or serving coffee. Perhaps coffee helps pay your bills, or someone else's bills in your family…

Thus, coffee is something that most of us can relate to as vital to our American standard of living. Now, imagine the global importance of coffee. In many coffee-producing countries along the equator, this bean is even more vital. In many developing countries, newly affluent entrepreneurs are adopting a coffee habit. In Russia, coffee is threatening to overthrow vodka as the drink of choice for the up-and-coming generation.

Needless to say, what happens to coffee impacts people at every level of society on every continent. In many ways, coffee is itself a petroleum product because it relies heavily on oil and gas to cultivate, harvest, transport, and brew. Because it's grown in environmentally sensitive areas, coffee also serves as a canary in the coal mine for the environment.

That's why I've chosen coffee as the lens through which we can understand the multitude of global crises that are brewing right this moment. This is truly a time unlike any other in history.

> *"History does not repeat itself, but it does rhyme."*
> – Mark Twain

When I hear someone droning on about history "repeating" itself, it's like nails on a chalkboard. The fact is that certain events do seem to repeat throughout history… until you actually study them closely. Then what you see is important themes and similarities, NOT repetition. That's like saying WWII was a repeat of WWI. Clearly, there were similarities, but there were different historical and political issues at stake in each specific situation.

Typically, what we see is nations struggling to stay afloat as their governments grow more excessive and burdensome until revenues unexpectedly dip. At this point, the government experiences a life-or-death crisis. Leaders get sucked into a dogfight to maintain political power, which they've become helplessly addicted to throughout their careers. Soon enough, they're ready to do anything to keep it.

This is precisely the situation that many governments around the world find themselves in today. Several times over the past few years, the United States has been on the verge of a massive financial cliff. Many other countries, including Greece, Cyprus, Iceland, Spain, and Egypt are in similar situations. Some of these countries have been teetering on the edge of insolvency.

All around the globe, sovereign nations are bailing out neighboring countries at a staggering pace. If these bailouts come to an end, because the creditor nations either can't or won't continue with their generosity, the results will be catastrophic. Governments that have been backed into a corner are dangerous, often starting wars with surrounding nations, declaring martial law, or both.

Consequently, the term bailout is an interesting choice for the situation at hand. It is a maritime term that means the act of removing water from a sinking ship, usually with a small bucket. The water returns more quickly than the bailout, meaning that the ship continues to sink. Recently, MIT released a study, which stated that according to their research, the entire world's economy will collapse by 2030. But what does this mean for you?

Consider this scenario:

Suburbia, United States of America

"No more coffee," James mumbled as he massaged his temples, trying to alleviate the intense explosions of caffeine withdrawal that were threatening to melt the eyes right out of his head. His caffeine supply of soda and coffee ran out two weeks ago, and two months before that the world had ended. Now his family faced total deprivation as their supplies ran out, their food supply was low, and the entire infrastructure around them had fallen apart.

In some ways, the end of the world had been a slow collapse. He hadn't realized exactly what was happening until complete disaster had already crossed the threshold from bad to worse, and then to destitute. After reflection and the keen vision of hindsight, he remembered the day the UN called a global state of emergency. The day it had become obvious to everyone that there was no turning back came when all entitlement spending stopped, resulting in mass rioting and chaos. However, it was obvious that the massive welfare state had been part of the initial problem. Government overreach, corruption, and bureaucracy had made much of the welfare state necessary in the first place.

James also wondered if the 9/11 attack on the World Trade Center had been the real cause for the current mega-disaster. When the Twin Towers fell, the official war began. Of course, that was nearly 15 years ago. Times had changed. There had been a lot of government backhandedness.

Over the previous decade, the government had amassed huge caches of weapons and ammunition. It had passed legislation that paved the way for martial law. Falsehoods and outright lies were well known to the public, and yet no one did anything about it. James assumed that was because they were all so comfy with their own personal lives filled with iPhones, reality TV, and fast food. As long as people still possessed all of their creature comforts, they didn't seem to notice what freedoms they were losing.

James believed that he had been just too busy to care about things that didn't seem to directly affect him at the time. Vaguely, he remembered hearing about riots and "frozen zones" in Brooklyn, but he assumed what he heard was merely rumor and not worth his time. Plus, there was no way that a frozen zone was anything like martial law. Work was hectic and there were bills to pay, social events to attend, and vacations to plan.

Damn, did he miss cheeseburgers. "Any manner of animal protein," he thought bitterly. Everything in his fridge and freezer had spoiled just a couple of days after the electricity had become unreliable. They had polished off the last of the fish last week. He grilled the cod on the barbeque they had pulled into the kitchen so as not to attract too much attention from their starving neighbors. He postulated that if they had owned a dog, they would have eaten it too. The food supply went down hard and fast about two months ago when the trucking companies couldn't pay their employees' wages, let alone the fuel costs it required to ship the much-needed foodstuffs. Looters swarmed the grocery stores immediately after the news broke. Within minutes, the shelves were empty.

Time for an Emergency Preparedness Reality Check

Could you and your family endure this bleak scenario? You may think of it merely as fiction, but here are a few facts that may change your mind:

- An event is a natural disaster if 10 or more people die or if 100 or more people find themselves homeless.
- According to Oxfam, the British charity, weather-related disasters are up 400 percent since the 1980s. These incidences are becoming increasingly severe and costly, putting a measurable strain on a country's economic growth and financial system.
- The IMF (International Monetary Fund) supplies emergency financial assistance to those who have suffered from natural disasters. One of their latest surveys stated that 700 natural disasters were reported in the last two years, affecting 450 million people.
- In 1925, the Tri-State Tornado killed 700 people in Missouri, Illinois, and Indiana.
- The Central China Floods of 1931 killed an estimated

3 million people.

- When Mount St. Helens erupted in 1980, 57 people were killed.

- The 1988 US Heat Wave killed nearly 10,000 people.

- In 2003, an earthquake in the Iranian city of Bam killed 40,000.

- Hurricane Katrina swept through the South in 2005. It was the costliest natural disaster in US history, causing 1,833 fatalities.

- The Waldo Canyon wildfire forced thirty-five thousand residents to abandon their Colorado Springs homes in 2012, as fire consumed 200,000 acres and 350 houses.

- The Colorado Floods in September 2013 killed 10 people, and caused nearly $2 billion in property damage. Over 10,000 people were evacuated across a stretch of 200 miles that were decimated by massive flooding.

Are you and your family prepared for such disasters? If you had to evacuate and flee your home this moment, what would you do? What would you take with you to help you survive? Do you have a plan in place for such an event? Even with careful preparation, plans can go awry during a true emergency, due to panic and other circumstances out of your control. Do you have a plan ***B***? Or even a plan ***C***?

Extreme weather is only the tip of the iceberg. Virtually all systems on planet earth are reaching their breaking point. We have a population overload that is overwhelming the resources available. Currently, humankind is using the resources equivalent to 1.5 planet Earths. If everyone were to achieve the lifestyle of the average American, the UN estimates that that number would increase to 3.5 Earths. We don't have two or three extra Earths in reserve. We simply don't have any other options but to walk this tightrope that we're on and hope for the best… but we can prepare for the worst.

By 2025, more than half of the world's population will be facing water-based vulnerability. Our supply of fresh water will be a severely limited vital resource, carefully allocated for hygiene, sanitation, and farming subsistence crops (read: not coffee). Oil demand is growing faster than it can be extracted and refined. Thanks to industrial farming, genetically modified plants are destroying native ecosystems and pesticide use runs rampant. Government budgets continue to expand while central banks devalue their currencies in a feeble attempt to manage their debts.

Preparedness is no longer a fringe hobby enjoyed by those with too much time on their hands. Even FEMA, the Federal Emergency Management Agency, recommends that everyone have a 72-hour kit with food, water, and other essentials for every member of your family, including the family pet. FEMA openly admits that it cannot respond to everyone immediately in a crisis. It can actually take up to 72 hours to mobilize resources and manpower.

Many experts in emergency management recommend 96-hour kits. Experts agree that a normal, healthy human can live up to about three weeks without food, IF they have potable water. Insufficient water is a much bigger problem. People can live only three days without water.

Case Study

To cite an extreme case, in 2011, a Swedish man survived from December 19th to February 17th with a very small amount of food, trapped in his car under the snow. The article reporting this story from the BBC states, "Experts believe it is possible for the human body to survive without food for up to two months." Theoretically, you can live eight weeks without food. However, this depends on environmental conditions, such as heat and cold, and on your own general health, including your emotional and mental well-being. Symptoms of hunger generally set in within just a few days.

This is not the hunger of missing breakfast, or the irritation of caffeine withdrawals, but the hunger symptoms that come when your body begins to beg for sustenance. According to a document published by the Royal Society of Medicine, signs of intense hunger include: weakness, confusion, diarrhea, irritability, cognitive impairment, and immune deficiency. As the days go on, other, more advanced symptoms will begin to present themselves: hallucinations, convulsions, muscle spasms, irregular heartbeats, and then DEATH.

If you have no food, you better hope you have drinkable water. Water is only second to oxygen on the list of necessities for life. Without water, your eyes and mouth become dry, your eyes will look sunken, and your kidneys will fight valiantly to preserve water, thus slowing down your urinary output.

Dehydration sets in. You become tired and dizzy as your physical strength decreases at a rapid pace. Confusion will start to get a foothold, as your brain, which is 70 percent water, begins to die. This develops into irritability, hallucinations, vomiting, and diarrhea. Your body's regulatory system will start to malfunction and you may even begin to sweat, expediting your already dire situation. You may even experience loss of movement and sensation in your arms and legs as your body shunts the much-needed fluids to your core in an effort to keep your heart beating.

Before you die of such advanced dehydration, your blood pressure will drop considerably, and you will experience an odd sense of disconnection from your body. You may even feel euphoric, or perhaps you'll be screaming inside. During this time, your skin will take on a bluish-gray color, as all the systems in your body will begin to systematically shut down. This is severe hypovolemic shock. And then you are DEAD.

It had been nearly two days since James and his family had any clean water to drink. Although he wasn't sure if he could consider the water they boiled out of the fish tank and toilet reserve tanks "clean." Their 30-gallon water heater had provided drinkable water for them in the beginning, but that well dried up quickly.

In the next room, James heard his wife, Mary, trying to comfort their two-year-old son Jacob. He was hungry, and the family only had a can of mini corns and half a jug of maple syrup left in the cupboard, neither of which was a fitting meal for a toddler. His chest felt tight as he listened for a moment to his son's sobs and whimpers, and the soft cooing as his wife tried to soothe the little guy. He felt responsible for the present situation; it was his own fault they were in such dire straits. For years, James threw away the fliers that were stuck to his windshield promoting emergency preparedness. At the time, he considered such notions to be in the arena of conspiracy theorists and loonies. Now, his immense regret made his empty stomach knot up, as he stood and checked through his small backpack for the many kitchen knives he had stored away for his upcoming mission.

He had to find food for his family.

Forty-eight hours ago, the family down the street tried to break in. He assumed they were looking for food or water, but James had no provisions to spare. He did not have a choice when he killed his neighbor Brad. He had let Brad's wife and her sister run away. He couldn't allow himself to cross the line by killing women. He had told his wife that Brad's death was an accident, and he had tried to convince himself of it for a time. Deep inside, he knew what he had been doing when he'd smashed the man's head over and over into the pavement. He only felt rage as he tried to protect his family. It was an animalistic fury he had never experienced before.

The dead body of the father of two, his long time friend, lay just outside his improvised fortifications, rotting in the July sun. He hadn't considered yet what to do with the body. He was revolted when he thought, "Maybe it'll attract food—cats, birds, or even mice." He could admit that the stray thought of cannibalism had crossed his mind, but it was only in the quickest of glimpses. He could not consider such an act with any serious thought.

Letting his chin come to rest in his palm, he leaned forward on the table and considered joining the militia that had formed. Their base was a few miles away and he thought he could get his family there. However, he wasn't enthusiastic about their tactics. Their motto seemed to be: Take everything, and screw everyone else. In fact, he had seen one of the men gun down an elderly woman who had tried to fight back when they pulled a decaying apple right from her hand. And as he thought about food for his family, his own morality slowly ebbed away. The old woman was of no use to the makeshift militia, but he was fairly young and able-bodied. He figured they had an 80 percent chance that the group would accept his family and a 20 percent chance that they would shoot them dead where they stood. Having never shot a gun before, James wondered how it felt.

The whole situation burned in his nose, and he scrunched up his face in irritation and disgust. The house smelled terrible, hell—the whole neighborhood smelled downright awful! The toilet sat passive, un-flushed for days. Weeks of garbage imitated a ghastly mountain outside. The smell of his son's diapers baking out on the street wafted into the house and burned his nostrils, giving an extra throb to his already pounding head. Wiping at his watering eyes, he couldn't decide if it was because of the stench, or if he was actually crying. "What a waste of water!" he thought. These desperate days had numbed James.

Chapter 1: Why Coffee Topples Empires

One year before the collapse...

James and Brad walked down Pinnacle Street, James carrying his infant son Jacob, and Brad toting his youngest daughter Emma. Brad's oldest, Lizzy, who was five, promenaded in front of them, randomly picking flowers along the sidewalk and shoving them into her dad's coat pocket. "These are for Momma," she stated very sternly to him before prancing off after another cluster of dandelions.

Brad laughed at his daughter's antics, "I'm sure your mother will love these."

His statement seemed to confuse her; she stopped for a moment and looked over her shoulder at him with a befuddled expression. "Why would she not?"

A rumbling of the ground interrupted any comeback he had. Brad and James looked at each other for a moment. "Earthquake?" James inquired. People began to poke their heads out of their front doors and draw curtains away from windows as the sound increased.

"Daddy?" Lizzy yelled, pointing down the street.

"Come here, Liz," Brad said, as he saw the first greenish-colored tank coming into view.

Lizzy moved herself safely between the two men, James saw another type of armored vehicle coming up behind the first and what looked like soldiers marching alongside it. "A parade!" Lizzy declared, clapping her hands in delight.

The Common Thread: Financial Crisis

No matter how it comes about, the collapse of most nations throughout history begins with insurmountable financial challenges. As I explained in the introduction, political leaders are addicted to power. When the threat of default places their power in jeopardy, these power junkies get backed into a corner. They must come up with a solution or face disgrace. This makes them wildly volatile, not to mention dangerous.

For this reason, a debt crisis has been a trigger point for massive unrest throughout history. A debt crisis requires politicians to make tough decisions, which, you'll see in the following examples, often destroy exactly what the politicians were trying to "save."

The American Revolution

In the time leading up to the American Revolution, the British Parliament was feeling the financial burden of defending its global empire. Determined to pass some of these costs along to the colonists, in 1767 Parliament passed a series of controversial taxes on basic necessities like stamps, sugar, and of course, tea.

Yes, it's hard not to notice the correlation between tea and coffee. In the British colonies, tea was still the drink du jour, and anyone or anything that got between a colonist and his tea was highly unwelcome. This line of thinking led to the "Boston Tea Party," where colonists dumped tons of tea into Boston Harbor. In retaliation to the protest and the destruction of the East India Company's tea, Parliament passed what became known to colonists as the "Intolerable Acts," which stripped Massachusetts of its right to self-government. You might say that this was a declaration of martial law.

You know the rest of this story, of course. The important takeaway is the almost unreasonably high value that the colonists placed on their daily necessities, especially tea. The British government's lust for a global empire left them in a difficult financial spot. They attempted to tax their way out by targeting those who didn't have any political representation, much less political power, and it lead to outright revolt in a matter of a few short years.

Does the Boston Tea Party or the Revolutionary War have anything to do with the fact that Americans now drink coffee instead of tea? It's fun to think about.

The French Revolution

When Louis XVI came to power in 1774, his nation was in desperate financial straits. Ironically, some of this came on account of helping the American colonists revolt against Britain, France's longtime rival. Apparently, French leaders thought making Britain look bad was worth putting the health of their own nation in jeopardy.

Not only was France facing crushing debt levels, but its system of taxation was heavily regressive. That is, the nobility and clergy in 18th century France enjoyed massive tax exemptions and paid very little in taxes. The commoners, on the other hand, owned next to nothing and thus they couldn't take advantage of the exemptions. These were the farmers who worked the land, but owned none.

The French, like the English, were trying to tax their way out of a debt crisis. As the situation grew more unsustainable,

Louis XVI allowed his ministers to change their tax policies, but it quickly became clear that there was no way out. Eventually, mobs began to form. The French Revolution began, leading to the beheading of Louis XVI and Queen Marie Antoinette.

The Collapse of the Ottoman Empire

The Ottoman Empire was famously described, by Tsar Nicholas I of Russia, as the "sick man of Europe." The Ottomans were far behind the rest of booming industrial Europe, and even lacked any rail system until late in the 19th century. In an effort to catch up to the rest of their neighboring countries, the Ottoman Empire instituted heavy taxes.

Again, the poor took the brunt of most of the taxation in the Ottoman Empire. Unfortunately, the poor were mostly an agricultural and farming population, so this demand weighed hard upon them. After the Crimean War, the Ottoman Imperial Bank was established by British and French financiers to provide a line of credit to the government, but I bet you can see where this is going.

With its broken economy and stifling taxes, the last thing the "sick man of Europe," needed at this point were easy credit and more debt. But it bears repeating that politicians will typically do anything to cling to power just a little longer. So that's what they did. The Ottoman government began defaulting on its interest payments in 1875.

By 1883, the British occupied the province of Egypt in an effort to control the public debt of the Empire. At the close of WWI, the creditor nations picked off the rest of the Ottoman Empire's territories. The British invasion took Mesopotamia, Palestine, Lebanon, and Syria. The Sykes-Picot agreement divided these lands between the French and British. Then in 1923, after occupation by Allied powers, the Ottoman Empire dissolved and was replaced by Turkey.

Fast Forward to Today

Just because we study history doesn't mean our leaders have the discipline or wisdom to truly learn from it. The truth is, several nations in the developed world are facing similar financial crises (including the US), just like the ones that brought down the British, French, and Ottoman Empire. History doesn't repeat, but it does rhyme.

The United States is currently experiencing similar events as those previously cited. We have been at war for 12 years and are severely in debt. As of March 22, 2013, the total outstanding public debt was $16,749,924,938,094.43. We usually just say $16.7 trillion so that the tremendous amount of digits doesn't seem so overwhelming. Our debt-to-income ratio is unbalanced and so far upside down that it's hard to even comprehend. In fact, the Federal Government has given up on the idea of confronting the problem, opting to hide its head in the sand.

Congress has failed to pass a federal budget for years now. They said the fiscal cliff would never come to pass, and yet it came and went. They raised the debt ceiling to give themselves time to negotiate a solution, but when the deadline came, there was no solution and they raised the ceiling again. We recently experienced a government shutdown, due to issues negotiating the federal budget. This period will certainly go down in history as one of the greatest examples of collective denial humankind has ever experienced.

Procrastination aside, the United States government is fully aware of the past and the coming future we may all face. However, instead of working hard to create a better future, they're preparing for the worst. On February 26th, Sarah Palin commented on her official Facebook page that the government is "stockpiling bullets in case of civil unrest."

An article in *Forbes Magazine* this year confirmed the Department of Homeland Security had purchased around 1.6 billion rounds of ammunition in 2012. They currently have a solicitation for another 200 million more rounds designed for use by snipers. This act is not even permissible during war times under the Geneva Conventions. However, the Department of Homeland Security sidestepped the Geneva Convention by referring to these stockpiles as "personal defense weapons."

On September 28, 2012, "H.R. 6566 (112th): Mass Fatality Planning and Religious Considerations Act" came before congress. It was referred to committee, and on December 27th, 2012, Representative Laura Richardson, the sponsor of the previous bill from California presented another bill entitled, "H.R. 6715 (112th): To authorize the Secretary of Homeland Security, acting through the Administrator of the Federal Emergency Management Agency, to make grants to State and local governments to assist in preparing for and responding to mass casualty incidents, and for other purposes." Since this was written, it has also been referred to committee. The Committee on Homeland Security and Governmental Affairs determined in a report on October 3rd, 2012 that there was no domestic terrorist threat.

Keep in mind, Homeland Security does not operate abroad, so the question becomes: Why are we preparing for mass fatalities if there is no domestic terrorist threat? The horrible truth is that Homeland Security is arming itself to the teeth in order to maintain political control against DOMESTIC unrest. Who are the targets for those bullets? Could the United States government be preparing for civil war?

While the US Government quietly stockpiles and prepares, state governments are militarizing their police forces. Here are a few examples:

- In the wake of the Boston Marathon bombing, the entire nation watched as all levels of government cooperated to shut down the entire city of Boston in the largest martial law effort in US history. Over 1 million residents were instructed to "shelter in place" by Gov. Deval Patrick as authorities searched for the bombing suspects.

- In July 2010, Don Braun, San Diego, California's former chief of police, approved the use of AR-15 platform rifles for officers. He did this without board approval or public discussion. These semi-automatic assault weapons have been used in at least seven campus incidents.

- In Jasper, Florida, with a population of only about 2,000, seven police officers serve the town. In 2002, the Pentagon transfer program put a military-grade M-16 machine gun into each of their hands.

- In Fargo, North Dakota, the police department spent $8 million to arm police officers with the grade of gear once reserved only for soldiers at war. Every officer is now equipped with a military-style assault rifle and Kevlar helmets. They also purchased an armored truck, complete with a rotating turret for $256,643 and "borrowed" a $154 million MQ-9 Predator B drone from Homeland Security in order to arrest a farming family who refused to return half a dozen cows who had wandered onto their land.

- In the county sheriff's department of South Carolina sits an armored personnel carrier named "The Peacemaker," complete with a turret machine gun. Sheriff Leon Lott insists "The Peacemaker" will save lives.

- In August 2013, two SWAT teams searched for a man suspected of stealing a bicycle and a cart full of merchandise from Wal-Mart, shutting down an entire neighborhood in Ft. Collins, Colorado.

- In California in 2011, police dispatched a SWAT team into the home of a woman who had defaulted on her student loans.

- The Police Chief in Paragould, Arkansas announced that the police planned to patrol the streets wearing full SWAT gear, carrying AR-15 assault rifles, and that they would stop anyone they wanted to for any reason, or no reason at all. The Chief commented that he expected most people stopped would be innocent of any crime, but claimed it was the civilian's responsibility to "prove" his/her innocence. Public outcry put a stop to this plan.

- In March of 2013, police put part of Brooklyn, New York into a "frozen zone." This assignment to a frozen zone was essentially the enactment of martial law. This was a reaction to protesters demanding justice for the slaying of a young boy by two plain-clothes police officers. Mainstream media either refused or was barred from reporting this incident.

The Next Tea Party

Because the US is currently facing a massive debt crisis, we know that the future of the government is anything but certain. We also know that instead of facing the financial crisis head on, the US government is simply preparing to crush civil uprisings. In other words, they're afraid. They've backed themselves into a corner and there's no telling what they'll do next. Whatever it is, chances are that everyday Americans will not like it…

One way our politicians are trying to deal with the current crisis involves intentionally devaluing the dollar. The Federal Reserve has formally stated that their goal is to devalue the dollar 33 percent in the next two decades. They believe this will create jobs. In the history of their "easements," this has never been proven true. Some argue that instead they will essentially steal 10 percent of American's hard-earned savings. (Forbes)

In other words, your cash will buy 33 percent less coffee in a decade if the Federal Reserve is allowed to go about its business uninterrupted. Will it be interrupted by demonstrations, perhaps a new Tea Party?

All revolutions start with a single event that galvanizes the opposition against the powers that be. In the American Revolutionary War, many point to the Boston Tea Party as the flash point that set the stage for an armed conflict. In the French Revolution, it was the Storming of the Bastille. In the Russian Revolution, it was an event known as "Bloody Sunday."

On January 22nd, 1905, soldiers of the Czar's Imperial Guard fired upon unarmed, peaceful demonstrators, killing 96 and injuring nearly 1,000. The demonstrators were marching to present a petition to the Czar Nicholas II, asking for reforms. Without warning, the event degenerated into violence and bloodshed, damaging support for the Czar's government and spawning many of the forces that would eventually overthrow the Czar.

Events like this only become more likely as the misery index of a nation increases. It only takes one overzealous protestor, or one police officer with an itchy trigger finger, in order to spark violence on a massive scale. Consider the Kent State shootings in 1970, when Ohio National Guardsmen killed four unarmed college students and wounded nine others. The decision to fire on the protesters didn't come from on high. Rather, it was a result of the decisions of a few stressed out guardsmen.

US Attorney General Eric Holder said in a letter on March 4, 2013, that the Obama Administration believes it technically could use military force to kill an American on US soil. (Senator Rand Paul's letter to John O. Brennan, Assistant to the President for Homeland Security and Counterterrorism.)

The Next Tea Party Could Be the Coffee Party?

So let me ask you a question: Do you think an event like this could happen again? Could a public demonstration about something as simple as coffee lead to an overreaction by authorities?

By now, I hope you're beginning to understand that almost any substantial changes in the American standard of living could trigger demonstrations that could bring about a destabilizing event. It could be coffee, gas prices, ObamaCare, or even the bank bailouts.

Using the backdrop of the Occupy Movement as an example, it's obvious how much the government fears mass protests. For example, the New York City Police Department has admitted that they deployed "counter-terror" measures against Occupy Movement protesters. In the dead of night, police officers in full riot gear entered Zuccotti Park in Manhattan and deployed a surprise invasion of the peaceful protestors' encampment, using klieg lights and a military-style sound machine. (ACLU)

The Posse Comitatus Act of 1878 bars the military from playing the role of law enforcement in the United States, however the Pentagon has made military equipment available to local police departments since the 90s for free, or close to free prices. This is a direct result of the passage of a bill passed in 1981 called the "Military Cooperation with Law Enforcement Act," which allowed police access to military bases, research, and equipment.

In 1994, another law passed that authorized the Pentagon to donate surplus military equipment to local police departments. The National Journal reported that just three years after the law was passed, the Pentagon distributed 3,800 M-16s, 2,185 M-14s, 73 grenade launchers, and 112 armored personnel carriers to civilian police agencies all across America. Spending on this type of military-style equipment has grown exponentially throughout the "War on Terror." A journalist studying the issue, Radley Balko, told a House subcommittee in 2007 that the use of SWAT teams in the last two decades has seen a 1,500 percent increase.

Can you imagine what might happen if these weapons were used, intentionally or accidentally, on unarmed protesters?

Numerous tipping points threaten to flip the United States into chaos. With the federal and state governments blatantly preparing for the worst, two questions arise: What will be the force that sends the country into free fall? Moreover, is the average American citizen prepared for the fallout?

One well-timed event could bring the most powerful nation in the world to its knees.

Two months after the collapse...

James had learned from previous excursions to avoid being out in the open during daylight. The first time he left to forage, he had ignorantly walked down the sidewalk at high noon. He had gone to the Atkinson's home two streets over to raid their garden. They had abandoned their home not long after the collapse, and he knew they had a small grow house in their basement that he and Brad had helped them put together a few years back. There hadn't been much left; looters had cleared out their cupboards already but had not known about the basement garden. Not much was there either, but he had been able to dig up a few potatoes from the large barrels in the corner. He had been walking home, with the potatoes in a plastic bag, when a handful of teens had jumped him and stolen the much-needed food.

He knew better now. He afforded himself a single glance at the corpse on the lawn before carefully squeezing through the cut chain-link that encompassed his own yard. It was easy to slip into his neighbor's backyard. He felt twitchy as he glanced up in search of drones and strained his ears for any sounds of life. He hadn't seen any in-person military presence since that day on Pinnacle Street. The military had informed them later that night that it had been an army training exercise. Howev-

er, the drones were a constant presence, and with them there wasn't any real need for actual soldiers. The gleaming white crafts were well-armed and possessed a deadly precision. He wasn't sure the purpose of their patrol, but he had seen a man shot dead by one for no reason that James could determine.

As it was now sunset, he hoped that the shadows would keep his presence hidden from any prying eyes. His goal tonight was to make it to the canal for water. He also remembered seeing a few fruit trees at one point that grew along its cement banks.

Moving forward, he made his way from one yard to the next as stealthily as he could. At the seventh house, a noise like the crinkling of paper caught his attention and he froze, pushing his back up against the cold stone wall behind him. The disturbance had stopped as quickly as it happened, and he shook with the effort needed to calm his pounding heart. His eyes darted in every direction as he tried to be quiet enough to find the source of the sound. James' eyes widened as he saw a man peeking over the fence with a flashlight, the butt of his rifle clearly visible over his wide shoulders. The man moved the beam of light in a swishing pattern. Fear stole the air from James's lungs as he willed himself to become part of the wall. There were several clay pots stacked neatly to his side, but he knew that they would not hide him well enough. He prayed. He prayed to a god in whom he no longer believed.

After several tense moments, the man left and James

gulped in several breaths of relief before continuing. Dashing through the last few yards, he came upon the canal. His face fell as he saw how empty it was. There was no water, but he gained a scrap of hope when he saw the waterspout. Hurrying, he climbed down the one side and up the other to the spout and grasped the wheel with both hands. The wheel was tight, but eventually it moved. Excitement rushed into him as the first small drops of water dripped down into the canal. Then there was nothing. His head fell in defeat as he dropped down on the ground next to the dry duct.

Looking up at the stars, James felt hopeless. Out of habit, he found the constellation Orion and traced its bow in the air. When he was little, his mother had told him stories of Orion, how he had been a fierce warrior and protector. She said Orion protected all the small children while they slept at night. As he came down towards the bottom of the bow, something odd caught his eye through the chain fence. At first it had looked like a cluster of dead bush and weeds, but a glint of orange caught his eye. Making his way closer, he quickly realized that tangled in the mess was a neglected tomato plant. Using his bolt cutters, he snipped through the chain-link and slipped into the yard. Kneeling before the bush, he pulled his backpack off and unzipped it, setting it in front of him as he carefully snaked his arms around the dead foliage and snatched the fruits out. They were small and nearly overripe, but he smiled knowing they were still edible. He contemplated eating one now, but felt that it would be wrong considering his family hadn't eaten yet.

When he was done with his harvesting, he stood and looked around the yard for a moment, realizing that he knew this house. This was George and Emmalyn's house. They had lived here with Emmalyn's parents long before he and Mary had moved into their home. He wondered briefly what had become of the multigenerational family before shrugging his pack back on and beginning his march home.

Chapter 2: Coffee as a Benchmark

Americans love coffee in almost any form: Hot, iced, black, or disguised by loads of sugar and syrup. The caffeine (known to scientists as 1,3,7-trimethylxanthine) in coffee releases dopamine, which makes you feel happy and optimistic. Coffee also stimulates the nervous system to increase concentration, decrease fatigue, and give you better memory. Although caffeine has its drawbacks, such as de-hydration and addiction, it offers some very attractive mental benefits.

Perhaps caffeine is the reason coffee has become a staple of the American diet, or maybe it's the flavor, or even the fact that it symbolizes "leisure" in many of our minds. The fact is, several of the fastest growing companies over the last two decades have made a fortune by selling coffee. If you're a commodity trader, this comes as no surprise.

Coffee is the second most widely traded commodity next

to oil. This precious bean is produced in over 60 countries, many of which are contained within an area of the globe known as *The Coffee Belt*, located between the tropics of Cancer and Capricorn. The coffee plant favors high elevations but doesn't tolerate freezing temperatures. The most favorable area to commercially produce coffee takes up a total of only 1 percent of the world's land mass. Thus, it is a relatively finite natural resource that, like oil, is experiencing an exponential growth in demand.

Coffee History and Folklore

According to coffee legend, the story begins in Ethiopia with a goat herder who noticed that his goats acted quite "playful" after nibbling on the berries of the coffee tree. The legend goes on to include a monk or a priest. In one version, it's a priest who comes across the goat herder and inquires about the man's odd goats. He then takes the berries back to his parish where he offers them to his followers as a way for them to stay awake during his extremely long sermons.

Another ending of this story has the goat herder bringing the berries to a monk, but the monk finds them to be against god and throws them into the fire. When he smells the aroma of the roasting beans, he rakes them out of the fire and throws them into water to preserve them. Unable to resist, he then tastes the brew and finds it to be pleasing.

Many stories revolve around the coffee plant. Supposedly, Sudanese slaves ate the fruit of the coffee plant, known as coffee cherries, in order to help them stay alive as they rowed ships across the Red Sea between Africa and the Arabian Peninsula. They took the plant from Sudan into Yemen and Arabia and then through the port of Mocha. By the 15th century, coffee was being cultivated in Yemen. However, in an attempt to prevent its cultivation elsewhere, the Arabs imposed a ban on the export of fertile coffee beans. The Dutch, who snuck live coffee plants back to their greenhouses in the Netherlands, eventually circumvented this restriction in 1616.

The first coffeehouses, known as "kaveh kanes," opened in Mecca. Coffee drinking was initially encouraged by the authorities of Yemen as an alternative to alcohol, which was and is still banned by their majority religion. These kaveh kanes spread quickly throughout the Arab world and thrived as places where chess was played, gossip was exchanged, and singing, dancing, and music were enjoyed. The Arabian coffeehouse soon became the center of political activity and was quickly suppressed. For the following few decades, coffeehouses and coffee itself was banned.

Murad IV, the sultan of the Ottoman Empire, made coffee drinking a capital offense. He would often dress in the garb of a commoner and walk the streets with a sizable sword, beheading anyone he saw drinking it. The issue kept reappearing, however, and eventually the ban lifted when tax on both the coffee and the kaveh kanes was enacted. Even in the Western world, coffeehouses have long been considered places where political and revolutionary discussions routinely take place.

As coffee spread into Europe and into the New World, a new wave of coffee consumption began to emerge. The first historical record of coffee consumption in North America was in 1668. Soon coffeehouses began to pop up in on Wall Street in New York, in Philadelphia, in Boston, and other towns. It was in a coffeehouse called the Green Dragon that the Boston Tea Party was planned. So it's safe to say that America and coffee have a long and meaningful history.

The Rise of the Coffee Trade

The Dutch brought the coffee plant into Central and South America starting with their arrival in Surinam in 1718. The plant now reigns supreme as the main continental cash crop and now accounts for over 50 percent of the export earnings. They also introduced the crop to Jamaica in 1730, where today the most famous and, by far, most expensive coffee grows in the Blue Mountains. In Brazil, sugar plantations, or "fazendas," owned by the country's elite began to be pushed out as sugar prices weakened and money and labor moved into the coffee business. By the 1830s, Brazil had become the world's largest producer of coffee, followed by Cuba, Java, and Haiti. As the coffee industry grew, the 20th century saw a continuous rise in demand for coffee, which led to even more expansion in production throughout the coffee-growing regions of the world. After World War II, many newly independent nations such as Uganda, Kenya, Rwanda, and Burundi found themselves in varying degrees of dependence on the revenue gained from exporting their coffee crop.

In 1963, The International Coffee Organization (ICO) was established in response to the first International Coffee Agreement (ICA) in 1962. Following a series of "agreements" between coffee producing countries, they created a *Coffee Study Group* to consider negotiating an agreement to include both exporting and importing countries. This helped prices remain stable from 1963 to 1972, strengthening the economies of the coffee-producing countries.

Coffee as an Economic Indicator

With the rise of Starbucks, coffee consumption reached a new status in the American economy. Instead of being something Americans brought at the grocery store and drank with breakfast, coffee became a fast food retail item, and a premium one at that.

These days, coffeehouses aren't the domain of arty college students, political activists, and intellectuals. Going out for coffee has now been absorbed into the routine of mainstream America. This has made it an excellent economic indicator through the last few periods of economic turbulence.

In addition to how much coffee is purchased through retail grocery chains, we now have access to data that tracks "Coffee Consumer Confidence" through the amount of coffee consumption outside the home. Sure enough, the amount of coffee purchased at Starbucks and other coffee establishments tracks closely along with economic factors like unemployment and recession.

For example, data from the National Coffee Association shows that coffee consumption outside the home fell from 40 percent in 2006 (just before the financial collapse) to a mere 27 percent in 2011. That's a massive decline that showcases how weak the supposed "recovery" has truly been.

"As consumers feel more comfortable with their jobs, it's not surprising to see people spend more on coffee outside of their home," said Ryan Sweet, a US economist for Moody's Analytics.

This is important, not only because coffee is a reliable indicator of economic health, but also because it predicts the health of the coffee retail economy. The coffee retail industry impacts millions of Americans directly through employment and indirectly through investments.

Because coffee is the second most widely-traded commodity on earth, the price of coffee will often reflect price inflation long before the Consumer Price Index (CPI), which the government uses to track inflation. Actually, a more accurate definition of the CPI is that it's an index that the government uses to tell us that inflation is not happening, even when it clearly is.

Threats to the Coffee Supply

Still, as the coffee industry matures, it continues to go through growing pains even today. Low coffee prices threaten the solvency of coffee producing nations across the globe. Coffee is still a massively valuable commodity, true. Its earnings are significant, staggering even, but the value of coffee beans as a commodity has not grown evenly.

In the 1980s, producing nations took in 20 percent of the profits from the coffee trade, while consuming nations retained 55 percent. By the late 1990s, the gap had widened to 13 percent for producers and 78 percent for consumers. As the coffee industry has grown tremendously in consuming nations (largely because of Starbucks), producer nations have struggled to make proportionate progress. Currently, the average coffee farmer receives approximately 41 cents per year for each coffee tree they maintain. So coffee isn't exactly a great cash crop.

By no means are low prices the only hardship facing coffee growers. New ecological challenges have begun to take their toll on the Coffee Belt. Coffee leaf rust began affecting coffee crops in 1976. Today the disease has a 53 percent incidence.

Some nations have declared an agricultural emergency in order to battle the epidemic, which caused an approximately 25 percent loss to total coffee production in 2012.

Many farmers have decided to abandon their coffee crops for more profitable crops. Khat is a common crop that Ethiopian people have begun to choose over coffee. It is a leafy narcotic that when chewed for a long time, makes people feel less hungry. Hunger is a huge issue in Ethiopia where over 11 million people face starvation. The new crop sells at nearly $200 a pound—whereas coffee is currently selling at $10 a pound in the US and $0.50 a pound on the world market. It also is drought and pest-resistant. Ethiopian officials state that this new surge in the semi-legal khat production is damaging their country's economy because it is part of the underground economy, and therefore, cannot be taxed.

This brings up a very good question: If you were a coffee producer making $0.41 per coffee tree in a nation like Colombia, wouldn't you consider a new crop? Perhaps something that you can sell on the black market and pay zero taxes on...

Other farmers in the Coffee Belt have abandoned coffee for corn. Corn is a crop that their government will actually pay them to grow through subsidies, because they can turn the corn into ethanol, which is now mixed into gasoline. This has created a familiar problem for the world. The overproduction of corn has severely depressed its price on the world market, and this forces farmers to plant less and less.

The result is less coffee on the market. As buyers begin to realize that there is no longer an abundance of coffee on the world market, prices will begin to climb steadily. Consumers are already losing purchasing power through the devaluation of the dollar, and just when things start to really get tough for the everyday American, the price of the second most widely traded commodity, coffee, (that they're dependent on) will rocket through the ceiling.

A coffee price spike would be felt through many parts of the US and global commodity market into a crisis, but coffee isn't the only agricultural good that's facing such a crisis scenario. Corn, sugar, beef, and many other crops are now barely viable thanks to oversupply and drought conditions. If farmers decide to throw in the towel, we will see an unprecedented global food crisis.

I can think of nothing that would get angry demonstrators out in the streets quicker than a food and caffeine shortage…

Two months after the collapse...

Returning home, James felt a sense of pride as he knocked on the back door. Mary appeared moments later, pushing open a gap between two boards. He smiled broadly at her, but the troubled look on her face caused a flood of panic to wash over him. "What happened?"

"We need to find a doctor." Her face was ashen. "There's something wrong with Jacob."

Dropping his plunderings to the kitchen floor, James dashed down the hall to his son's room. Jacob lay quietly in his bed, staring blankly at the ceiling. "Jakey?" he whispered, lifting his son from the crib.

Mary was near tears as she struggled to explain what had transpired since James' absence. "He... he stopped crying after you left. He just went limp." She sniffed and took a deep breath before continuing, "He stopped doing anything. He just... he just lies there."

James held his son tightly against him and looked helplessly at his wife, his mind racing for a solution. "He needs a doctor," she whispered.

"There are no doctors. There's not even an emergency room anymore." He couldn't speak louder than a whisper, his voice strangled.

"No... there are no doctors," she paused, "but there IS an emergency room."

James' voice could not hide the powerlessness he felt, "But there's no one there who can help."

"There's nothing else to do. We have to go. We have to try. Maybe there will be something." James nodded, and Mary grabbed a blanket from the crib and motioned for James to give Jacob to her.

"We have to go now. It's only a couple of miles," she said, wrapping the cloth snugly around the child.

They ran most of the way, darting from shadow to shadow. They didn't have the time to be as careful as James was on his earlier journey; their son's life was in distress. Unknown to them, they were being watched as they sprinted across the parking lot and through the unhinged doors of the emergency room. The ER was a mess, papers and what may have been blood splattered everywhere. Everything was gone. There weren't even hospital beds. James cradled his son tightly against his chest.

The unknown watcher entered the disheveled department and stood a moment, watching the couple and their child. "You look like you need help." His voice was gruff and startled the parents as they spun about face to see the man behind them. The man spread his hands before them, his palms out in a gesture of peace. "My name is Monroe."

Chapter 3: Economic Turmoil

James smiled sleepily at the image of his wife cradling their son as she sat cross-legged on the floor across from him. He glanced to the side as Monroe appeared in the doorway. "He'll be needing a change out soon," the taller man stated, lifting a clear, fluid filled bag for emphasis. James nodded and scooted down to the ground, next to his wife and son. Monroe sat down next to him and began fiddling with the long tube that ran from the old bag and into a needle stuck in the top of his son's hand.

"He seems to be doing better," James said, caressing the side of his son's face with the back of his hand. "He's not nearly so pale anymore."

Monroe finished his task and looked down at the toddler, setting two fingers against the inside of the child's upper arm. "He does seem to be better, but we should know for sure by morning." Monroe stood and gestured for James to follow him down the hall. They came to a makeshift kitchen area, and Monroe set two thin metal cups on the counter. "Coffee?"

It was just one word, but it seemed to have so much meaning. James nodded blankly as Monroe filled the cup and pushed it towards him. He held the warm liquid in his hands, staring into the rich darkness of it. He sipped it slowly and suddenly felt... human.

To sustain a healthy, growing economy with ample employment, most economists believe that America's GDP needs to grow at a rate over 5 percent each year. So where does that put us, in the context of this so-called "recovery?" Over the last 15 quarters, US GDP growth has averaged a miserable 2 percent, less than half of what we need to get back to "healthy" status. As the period of slow growth rolls on, the government is beginning to realize that the unprecedented stimulus programs not only failed, they also made massive sectors of the economy dependent on subsidies.

With this in mind, it's no wonder that unemployment has remained at historic levels and that millions of Americans have opted to leave the workforce and go "on the dole." While the official numbers out of Washington put unemployment at a high, however not unprecedented, 7.8 percent, this number doesn't reflect how many Americans have simply stopped looking for work.

True to form with most government logic, once you've officially stopped actively searching for a job, you're no longer unemployed. But those people, many of them in the prime of their working years, have not disappeared, as the government's calculations assume. Official figures from the Bureau of Labor Statistics (which always tend to skew to the positive) puts the number of Americans ages 24 to 54 that are not working or looking for work at 23.1 million. Not only are these people unemployed during their most productive years, they aren't even counted in the official unemployment numbers. With the workforce participation rate in the gutter, that simply means more Americans that need welfare assistance, more Americans who aren't able to save money, and more workers with outdated skill sets.

The Natives Are Getting Restless

With this information as the backdrop, it's easy to see why emotions bubble over with every passing controversy. Why do so many people march in the streets, "occupy" public property, and incite riots at the drop of a hat? The answer is that they simply have nothing better to do, no prospects, and they're not happy about it. Wouldn't you be?

As these demonstrations grow more and more common, the chances are greater that something will go wrong. It's been over a decade since we've witnessed major rioting in the United States, but it's been going on for several years in Europe. How have our leaders managed to keep the "melting pot" from boiling over?

Thanks to our nation's status as the world's greatest economic power, and the holder of the world's reserve currency, politicos in the US have a tool that their counterparts around the world don't have: The Federal Reserve. Because the world currently still depends on the dollar for trade, the government can inflate the currency supply without immediate repercussions. They've been able to avoid making decisions about austerity measures, kicking the can down the road while spending trillions of freshly printed dollars to keep the charade going.

If you want to know how bad the economy truly is, consider the Federal Reserve interest rates. They've been at 0 percent since the financial collapse in 2008. Bankers are not stupid; they don't lend money at zero interest because they're nice people. They do it because there's very little demand for their money.

The Lost Generation

For many older workers, hoping to retire in the next 5-10 years, the employment collapse was devastating. Many in this generation are angry at having to accept a lower standard of living, working through their retirement years at a low-paying, menial job. This generation watched its dreams get crushed under the weight of the housing bubble, financial collapse, and the bank bailouts.

There's another generation that is even more troubling to those in power, however. That's the younger generation of Americans who are reaching adulthood in a society where opportunities are scarce. Many of this generation are graduating from college with immense student debt (subsidized and encouraged by the government) but can't find a job that allows them to make the payments.

According to the government's Household Survey, a whopping 557,000 of the 753,000 jobs created in the first half of 2013 were part-time positions. The number of part-time jobs in America is at an all-time high, 3 million more that in 2007 when the recession began.

In June of 2013, for example, 75,000 of the 195,000 new jobs were created at restaurants and bars where the average paycheck is $351. The sad irony here is that the current generation that's emerging from college in massive debt is working at coffeeshops, trying to pay off their debts and survive with these meager wages.

The employment economy is depending more and more on the hospitality industry. But at this rate, who's going to be able to afford to buy a $5 cup of coffee or dinner at a nice restaurant? As this situation worsens, you can expect more rioting, more unemployed youth revolts, and welfare spending that the US government can't afford.

Chapter 4: The Cost of Coffee

Six months before the collapse...

Setting his frothy cup of gourmet cappuccino onto the end table, James sat down in his favorite plush recliner and snatched up his tablet. In the background, he vaguely registered the morning news reporting yet another riot in some New York slum, as he switched on the device and logged into his bank's website. Stretching, he leaned back into the chair and opened his statements. A quiet pride swelled in his chest as he glanced over his balances. Christmas would be good this year; he was looking forward to getting that new iPhone that was coming out in a few months.

The term "consumer" comes from the Latin term *consumo*, which means "to eat up completely." Unfortunately, the word sums up the attitude of most Americans today. Through industrialization and technology, we've become mostly a nation of consumers that don't produce much. Our lifestyles are amazingly convenient, that's true, but this convenience has come at a price. That price is the loss of our self-reliance.

Almost everything we do now depends on unseen systems that we don't control. Most people in the developed world are only vaguely aware of the logistical systems that make their lives possible. Massive supply chains and industrial farming operations bring food, produce, and coffee to the store for us to buy at our leisure. Something as simple as a long-term power outage could throw this system offline.

Why the Coffee Industry MUST Crater

We've already discussed some of the very serious trends that are threatening the American standard of living, things like unemployment, crushing debt, and stagnant wages. As these trends continue, they will threaten the viability of entire sectors of the economy. In keeping with the theme of this book, we're going to zoom into how this affects coffee.

First, let's start with the driving force behind coffee's rapid expansion into the retail economy: Starbucks. Since its inception in 1971, Starbucks has successfully brought coffeeshop culture to markets that no one ever believed would support such an enterprise. Starbucks's growth in North America has reached a plateau, however. For Starbucks, the next challenge is to maintain profitability in a changing consumer landscape. With fewer workers finding full-time jobs, and much fewer jobs overall, they've got their work cut out for them.

Let's take a look at the economics behind Starbucks. According to a case study, 21 percent of its customers make an average of 18 visits per month. Now Starbucks doesn't publish average ticket values, but a widely published survey in 2002 put the total for "highly satisfied" Starbucks customers at $4.42, while a "satisfied" customer paid on average $4.06. From this information, we can estimate that a highly satisfied customer visited paid an average of $4.42 on roughly 18 times per month, a total of $79.56 per month, $956.72 annually. And that was in 2002. If you've visited a Starbucks recently, you've probably noticed that $4.42 seems rather low based on their current menu.

A thousand dollar a year habit is hard to justify when you're on unemployment, or you're struggling to make student loan payments while working part-time at a restaurant.

Prices Nosedive and Quality Follows

As a consumer-driven society, prices in the US must follow wages and earnings. When the economy is growing at a healthy rate, citizens have more expendable income and can afford more luxury items. During a historically weak recovery, like we're in currently, retailers are under great pressure to keep prices low at all costs.

If Wal-Mart sells coffee at a lower price than another retailer, then Wal-Mart gets more sales. Eventually, competitors must match these prices or lose customers and face failure themselves. So who's going to make up the difference? Perhaps the better question is: Who will notice the difference?

In many countries of the Coffee Belt, coffee farmers can only afford so much labor because their product sells at such reduced rates. If coffee prices fall in the consumer economy, coffee prices in the commodity market will follow on a downward trajectory. A coffee farmer facing these lower prices has to consider cutting costs and lowering quality to keep business going. Instead of picking the ripe coffee cherries three times and year, they only pick them once and the product becomes a mix of ripe and unripe coffee beans. This action lowers the quality of their blends; which lowers the satisfaction with the product even more, and the entire commodity enters into a death spiral.

There is a deep correlation, as shown by the coffee laborers, between price and quality. Most of us understand this to be true in our own professional experience. There is even a saying that expresses this: "You get what you pay for." What we fail to realize is that not only do we get what we pay for, but the price at which we purchase products can destabilize an industry.

For example, if the price of coffee gets so low that it's impossible to make a profit, many farmers would simply find a new crop to grow or find a new business. This would send major ripples through the commodity market, many of which would not be felt until the next harvest season, far too late for any corrective action.

The concept that we all "live downstream," both figuratively and literally, is not a new idea, yet it is one of the most commonly forgotten. What we do affects others around the nation and around the world. For some time now, we have been aware that the overuse of antibiotics leads to superbugs. This has led doctors to become more stringent when prescribing this miracle cure. However, 85 percent of the antibiotics sold in the United States are for agricultural use. Many cows, pigs, chickens, and other livestock receive a daily dose of antibiotics. This keeps them relatively healthy and fattens them up for market.

This practice has a direct correlation to price affecting quality. Because purchasers demand a low price for milk, a farmer cannot afford to lose a cow to sickness or have his cow worth less in any way. Therefore, he gives his cows antibiotics and other treatments to keep them disease-free and plump. You can see this price difference when you go to the market and see the difference between regular milk and organic (no antibiotics) milk. In general, organic milk costs two to three times as much.

Our consumer culture makes little differentiation between want and need. We do not *need* a Starbucks caramel macchiato every day. We do not *need* an iPhone 5 or 6 or 42. You may *want it*, and it may make your life easier is some ways. Nevertheless, these items are not necessary for survival. Even *Forbes Magazine* commented on this issue and suggested that we look hard at the products we are buying as "wants or needs."

The Link Between the Economy and Government

When employment falls, prices fall, real estate values fall, and tax revenue falls. It's a domino effect that can very quickly spiral out of control. Consider the city of Detroit as an example.

Although most Americans have been too absorbed in their own lives to notice it, residents in Detroit are experiencing a very mild dose of what it's like to live in a failed state. In fact, you could say that Detroit is a microcosm of what will happen if and when the Federal Government is forced to declare bankruptcy by its creditors.

Consider a few of the facts of life for Detroit residents:

- 136,000 crimes were reported in 2011, most were for property crime, theft, and burglary.

- Unemployment is at 18.6 percent (that's the official number, the real figures are likely much worse).

- Average police response time to emergency calls is 58 minutes. (I bet if you asked the average Detroit resident, they would tell you that they've had to make a self-reliant home defense plan.)

- The entire city has only 26 fire engines, making the possibility of an out of control, city-wide fire a distinct possibility.

- Only 40 percent of the city's streetlights are operational.

Compared to the rest of the nation, Detroit is in a dire situation; a veritable third-world system surrounded by first world systems. Yet, in a very strange way, Detroit residents are ahead of the rest of us in two major ways.

1. Unlike the rest of the country, Detroit residents no longer have the illusion that all is well and that the systems that support their way of life are flawless and failsafe. For Detroit residents, the "it can't happen here" mentality has been shattered. They no longer have the feeling of safety that the rest of America may get from dialing 911.

2. Because simple city services can no longer be relied on, from trash collection to police response, Detroit residents are learning to become resourceful. Even if they never desired to or intended to, they're learning

to become self-reliant, both as individuals and communities.

Two months after the collapse...

James couldn't believe the turnaround in their circumstances. At their home, their son was getting sick, they were out of food and water, and everything reeked of disaster. Being in the hospital with Monroe opened his eyes to what he should have done long before the collapse. James wished he had been as prepared as Monroe was. It wasn't that the other man was overly prepared like the stereotypical doomsayer; it was the little things. Although there was one thing that was not so little: his medical training. Monroe was a certified EMT. When he had explained it to James, it didn't seem like it had been too terrible to become one either. A few months and a thousand dollars, and Monroe had the ability to save his son. It was something that James realized he could have done himself. Monroe had even explained about other emergency programs that were shorter and even less work. He had first been just another person who had taken a simple CPR course, and after that had taken a few weeks to become a first responder and learn about first aid.

Beyond the medical training, Monroe also had a pantry in his downstairs that was filled with freeze dried food and water. He had even more water in big blue barrels in his garage. There was also a small closet in the same room that contained other items such as medical supplies, toilet paper, candles, and camping equipment. He said that he hadn't bought everything at once, just accumulated it over the last several years. It all seemed so easy that James felt nearly embarrassed that he hadn't done "something."

Monroe explained that his crown jewel of preparedness was his truck, which James had found odd until he explained it. Apparently, Monroe had convinced the fast food companies nearby to give him their drippings instead of contracting with the local waste management center. He filtered the waste into biofuel and used the rest for candles. His 1992 Dodge pickup ran on the biofuel, leaving him no need for gasoline. Monroe had two 50 gallon barrels of fuel that he had strapped into the bed of his truck.

Chapter 5: The Decline of Earth's Resources

One week after the collapse...

"This is ridiculous!" James exclaimed, slamming the front door behind him and throwing his car keys across the room. "All the goddamn stores have been cleaned out! And the line for the gas pumps is nearly two miles long! You'd think people thought it was the damn apocalypse!"

"It'll be fine," Mary said soothingly as she picked up the discarded keys and set them gently on the end table. "I'm sure everything will be sorted out in a few days. We can survive until then."

Staggering population growth is putting the squeeze on resources of all kinds. Not only are more people competing for the same commodities around the world, but the shared resources, like water and air quality, will continue to slide as we struggle to meet the demands of an overpopulated planet.

According to the UN's latest projections, the world's population, just over 7 billion right now, will reach 9.6 billion by 2050, and 11 billion by the end of the century. Yes, fertility rates in most developing countries have been declining since the 1960s, but that's not offsetting the exponential growth in the developing world. Take Nigeria for example, a nation roughly the size of Texas, is on pace to overtake the US as the world's 3rd most populous country by 2050 and to rival China's population by the end of the century. Nigeria is just one example, of which there are many more.

There's no two ways about it, rising populations put pressure on the ecosystems they depend on. This isn't some alarmist mumbo jumbo; it's just simple math. We can improve crop yields to a point, but we can't manufacture water. The simple fact is that we're on the way to a tipping point. According to projections, once the earth's landmass becomes more than 50 percent tarmac and agriculture, the result will be global crisis. If the world hits this tipping point, Professor Anthony Barnosky of the University of California-Berkeley warns, "It really will be a new world, biologically, at that point."

The most recent data suggests that in just a few generations, if not sooner, there will be a reduction in biodiversity so severe that much of what we depend on to sustain our quality of life will disappear, including fresh water. Studies done on small-scale ecosystems have shown that once man alters 50-

90 percent of an area, the entire ecosystem tips irreversibly into a state far different from the original, and the result is the extinction of many of the species in that area.

The Ecological Tipping Point

Currently, humans have altered 43 percent of the earth's land surface to agricultural or urban use. By 2025, estimations show this figure will rise to 50 percent. Elizabeth Hadly from Stanford University said:

> "We may already be past these tipping points in particular regions of the world. I just returned from a trip to the high Himalayas in Nepal where I witnessed families fighting each other with machetes for wood—wood that they would burn to cook their food in one evening...In places where governments are lacking basic infrastructure, people fend for themselves, and biodiversity suffers. We desperately need global leadership for the planet Earth."

According to the United Nations:

- More than 3.4 million people die each year from water, sanitation, and hygiene-related causes. Nearly all deaths, 99 percent, occur in the developing world.

- Lack of access to clean water and sanitation kills children at a rate equivalent to a jumbo jet crashing every four hours.

- Of the 60 million people added to the world's town and cities every year, most move to informal settlements, like slums, with no sanitation facilities.

- 780 million people lack access to an improved water source, approximately one in nine people.

- The water and sanitation crisis claims more lives through disease than any war claims through guns.

- An American taking a five-minute shower uses more water than the average person in a developing country slum uses for an entire day.

- Over 2.5 times more people lack water than live in the United States.

- More people worldwide have a mobile phone than a toilet.

- Over the past 40 years, the world's population has doubled. Our use of water has quadrupled. Yet the amount of water on Earth has stayed the same.

- Less than one percent of the water on our planet is safe for humans to drink.

- About two percent of the world's fresh water is locked up in ice.

- Seawater is only good to drink for humans who live near the sea and can afford the cash and energy to desalinate it.

- Desalinated water costs 15 times more than regular water. It burns polluting fossil fuel energy, as solar powered desalination is in its infancy.

Eventually, most places will have to live with the water they have, if they have any. As underground supplies run dry, water shortages set in. Some countries are even attempting to mine fossil H2O that seeped into the rocks during the last ice age. The UN has determined that large parts of Africa, Asia, and Europe are already facing water stress or scarcity.

Sana'a, Yemen is one of the most water-stressed cities on Earth as two million people fight to get water from tankers.

Like most developing countries, agriculture uses 90 percent of water. In Yemen, the cultivation of khat, the narcotic many now grow, instead of coffee, uses the most water.

In America, Las Vegas pays its residents to dig up their lawns to save water. In the UK, civil engineers want to introduce a sliding tariff so people who water their lawns or wash their cars often will have to pay more. Who knows if this stuff will even work, but clearly these are different governments across the world from one another trying to deal with the same problem.

Agriculture consumes the lion's share of water in most countries, as it should. However, farmers decided what crops to plant based on how profitable they are, not how much water they use. Coffee is not a relatively high water-use crop, but as prices continue to remain low, many farmers will turn to other crops that take much more water, just as the farmers in Yemen have started growing khat instead of coffee.

The shortage of oil is a known issue to most people, but few people are aware of the future scarcity of some chemical elements. Although not well known, the shortage of certain elements will have a noticeable effect on our way and quality of life. According to the United States Department of Energy, the global demand for rare earth elements grew by a factor of about five from 1980 to the present.

There are 17 rare earth elements, which include all lanthanides plus yttrium and scandium. Mechanics and electronics use these elements the most. These are called rare not because they are scarce, but because it is difficult to find them in a high enough concentration that it is profitable to extract them.

Dysprosium, a metal, is one of the most rare earth elements. According to a 2012 review published in *Energy*, the demand for this element has significantly increased its price. The manufacture of permanent magnets is one of the top uses. Adding dysprosium ensures that the magnetic properties remain unaltered even at high temperatures. This makes the magnets suitable for applications such as: electric vehicles, wind turbines, and industrial motors. Currently, China mines 99 percent of this element. China has expressed the intent to reduce their exports of rare earth; to continue the supply of dysprosium, development of new mine projects will need to begin.

We use phosphorus for a variety of purposes, primarily in the production of fertilizers, but also in the production of food additives and rust-prevention products. Phosphorus is not yet a scarce element, but a study published in *Nature* in 2009 indicated that reserves of this element will vanish in approximately 50 years if our current rate of use continues. Recently, the price of phosphorus has increased due to geographical issues. For example, one of the mines located in China was severely affected by the 2008 earthquake in the Sichuan Province, and this caused the supply to fall and prices to rise.

The Coming Global Food Shortage

Agriculture has been and will continue to be the most hit by these resource shortages. Due to the government-subsidized demand for ethanol and the drought that has recently gripped the Midwest, the price of corn has doubled since 2009. The record-high prices are encouraging cattle farmers to feed their cows candy instead. The candy-feed consists of everything from gummy worms and ice cream, sprinkles to marshmallows, and chocolate bars not fit for human consumption or sale. Ki Fanning, a livestock nutritionist with Great Plains Livestock Consulting, said, "It is a very good way for producers to reduce feed cost and to provide less expensive food for consumers." Another livestock nutritionist, Chuck Hurst, of Nutritech, has said that the candy provides "the same kind of energy as corn." Farmers are offering their cows a wide assortment of not only candy, but also by-products and other foods such as soda crackers, cherry juice, fishmeal, peanut butter, fruit fillings, tapioca, and leftover grain from distilleries.

The United Nations has warned that world grain reserves are so dangerously low that severe weather in the United States could trigger a major hunger crisis. Failing harvests in the United States, Ukraine, and other countries have eroded reserves to their lowest levels since 1974. The US grain reserve currently holds a historically low 6.5 percent of the maize that it expects to consume in 2014. The food consumption of the world has exceeded the amount grown for six of the last 11 years, and countries have run low on their reserves. In 2008, the shortfall in the reserves started riots in 25 countries. Economists from around the globe warn that the global food supply system could collapse at any point, leaving hundreds of millions of people hungry.

At the beginning of 2013, NOAA—the National Oceanic and Atmospheric Administration—released their annual spring outlook report. They predicted hotter, drier conditions across much of the United States, including parts of Texas, Oklahoma, and Kansas. These are the exact places where farmers have already been fighting to hang onto their winter wheat crops. Some farmers decided not to bother to plant winter wheat. The three-month forecast noted weather hazards for the Midwest. It included heavy, late snows setting up conditions for flooding along the Red and Souris rivers, including approximately 20,000 acres of farmland in the Devil's Lake area in North Dakota. Reports also show indications of flooding along the upper Mississippi into southern Wisconsin, northern Missouri, and parts of South Dakota and Iowa.

The report continued on to say that California, the Southwest, the southern Rockies, and Texas will likely continue to experience drought conditions, and that the Florida panhandle, of all places, should expect the same. Increased and sustained drought conditions not only starve the country's crops of much needed water, but increase the risk of wildfires.

As if water scarcity weren't enough, scientists have begun to theorize new possibilities of global warming. These include:

- The spread of **disease** as northern countries warm and disease-carrying insects migrate north. Some scientists believe that global warming is the reason malaria has not been fully eradicated.

- More **hurricanes** as the temperature of oceans rise. Evidence of this has already presented itself with the stronger and more frequent hurricanes of 2004 and 2005. Hurricane strength has increased 50 percent in the last 30 years.

- The increasingly violent hurricanes will drain the **economy** as they cause billions of dollars in damage.

- **Rising sea levels** could cause enormous coastal flooding. Scientists theorized that if the 5,773,000 cubic miles of water in all the glaciers, ice caps, and permanent snow were to melt today, the seas would rise 230 feet.

- Melting ice caps will **desalinate** the ocean and manipulate the Gulf Stream that regulates the world's temperatures.

- **Smog-related deaths** will rise, as a hotter climate tends to lead to an increase of ozone.

- **Earthquakes** will increase in frequency as the glaciers melt and tectonic plates lose pressure. This can also bring about an increase in **volcanic activity**.

- As changes in climate and environment take hold, **animal attacks** will become more frequent as they move from their natural habitats in search of food.

Desertification and a return to the 1930s Dust Bowl seem possible futures for the United States. Increases in evaporation, accompanied by severely decreased rainfall could potentially lead to a barren wasteland that would be impossible to recover from. In the 1930s, poor farming practices and drought led to the Dust Bowl effect. Farmers plowed down the prairie grasses to make room for wheat farming. Unfortunately, a drought killed the crop and left utterly bare land. This caused catastrophic dust storms to ravage the areas, bringing hunger and even lung illnesses. Over three million people had to abandon their farms and move on.

No food. No water.

To tie this back into coffee, consider the sheer volume of milk that Starbucks uses in a year: 93 million gallons. If an average dairy cow produces 7 gallons of milk per day, that would require well over 36,000 dairy cows working at maximum capacity just to keep Starbucks making lattes. Can you imagine how many acres of land it takes to sustain 36,000 cows? In a drought?

Agriculture is Hanging by a Thread

The United States government subsidizes many crops, including corn, that require lots of water to grow. Unfortunately, the drought is causing significant issues. Moving away from government supported crops is risky, creating an incentive to stick with corn and other thirsty crops, and increase irrigation and fertilization to offset the dry weather.
One way the government, in its infinite benevolent "wisdom," subsidizes farming is through ethanol quotas. Most ethanol is made from corn, because corn is widely available, which supports overplanting. As the drought pushes crop yields down, farmers plant more to offset. And now that corn is both a food and a fuel, you can imagine how this affects food prices.

Activists and scientists alike warn that the US Government's current biofuel policies will only exacerbate the already critical situation. There are many people who question whether or not using corn for fuel is worth it, considering the rise in food prices. About 13 percent of global corn production is used by the United States for biofuels. Corn is one of the United State's top exports, and many impoverished nations worldwide rely on US corn imports to feed their masses.

The scorching temperatures and lack of rain have decimated American crops such as corn, wheat, and soy.

Not only has the United States suffered because of drought, but Russia, India, and Africa have also lost wheat crops. Corn is the primary staple in Africa and Central and South America. In South Africa the cost of corn has increased by more than 40 percent.

When food prices rise to such a level that people are unable to afford the basic necessities, people go hungry, and that hunger feeds into social instability and violence. In 2007 and 2008, food shortages in Haiti, the Philippines, and Bangladesh caused massive rioting. The United States has yet to experience food shortages, but you can bet that when prices spike, demonstrations could get very heated.

Populations in first-world countries only spend 10 to 20 percent of their income on food, but those in Third World nations spend up to 80 percent. According to Oxfam, a rise of only 1 percent in the price of food would result in 16 million more people crossing the threshold into impoverishment. Between 2007 and 2009, there were a reported 60 official food riots worldwide. The International Food Policy Research Institute in Washington warned that a global crisis could be just at our doorstep. The explosive combination of economic, energy, and environmental crisis is ready to detonate.

Across Colombia, coffee growers are in outrage as they drop

to the 4th largest coffee producer. They are blocking roads and demanding government aid. Anti-riot police have already injured dozens. The organizers have promised that the protests will continue indefinitely.

In 2012 Colombian coffee growers recorded the lowest coffee output in three decades. Their output consisted of only 7.7 million 132-pound bags of coffee; in 1992, it had been twice as much. Heavy rain, crop disease, and a seriously overvalued national currency have caused much heartache and misery. In fact, two out of every three cups of coffee brewed in Colombia are from beans from Peru and Ecuador, which historically have produced a much poorer quality bean than Colombia.

Coffee prices unfortunately keep dropping, and most farmers work on a small-scale. For these small-scale farmers, this means that they don't always have the means to handle crop loss like a large producer can.

Take Action for Your Survival: Building a Home Garden

In your own situation, is it possible to supplement some of your nutritional needs by growing some of your own food? Even in limited space, there are many options, even hanging upside-down growers such as for tomatoes and strawberries. Save your bottles and milk jugs and create a fantastic hanging garden. There are even types of vegetables that grow in small areas, such as the bush cucumber.

City foraging can also be a fun activity and a useful survival skill. The following are examples of edible plants found just outside your front door:

- Dandelion: This common weed is entirely edible from root to flower.

- Burdock: A good source of dietary fiber, calcium, and potassium.

- Lamb's Quarter: The leaves can be used as a replacement for spinach. The seeds are also edible and a good source of protein and vitamin A.

Survival Tip: Satisfied is good enough. Better three meals than one feast.

Three months after the collapse...

James dozed happily in his cot, listening to the first sounds of morning. He had to admit, without all the normal sounds of humanity, nature had quite a bit to say in the morning. A loud crash broke the peace and he sat straight up, startled. He saw from his peripheral vision that his wife had done the same and was clutching their son to her chest. Moments later, Monroe burst into the room and thrust a pistol into James's hands. "It's the militia!"

Chapter 6: The Geopolitics of Potential Societal Collapse

Two weeks before the collapse...

Traffic had come to a standstill and James was quickly losing patience. He had been in the wondrous state of not moving for the last thirty minutes. Turning the car off, he stepped out of his car to see if he could get a look at what was going on. Looking around, he noticed others were doing the same. Looking down the road, he saw the source of the chaos. What looked to be dozens, if not hundreds of people, were blocking the road not too far ahead. They carried signs and he could hear the muffled sounds of yelling, but he couldn't make out what they were saying or read the signs.

He heard sounds like loud firecrackers and ducked back into his car, pulling the door closed with a slam. Fear and panic prickled against the back of his neck as smoke quickly flooded in around the stopped cars. The haze and commotion seemed to go on for hours. People ran by his car and he could hear distant screaming. He knew this had to be a terrorist attack. Perhaps Al-Qaeda or some other group. Of course, that didn't explain the obvious protesters that he had seen.

And then the cars were moving again, and he could see police in SWAT gear guiding the cars to turn around. He didn't question; he just followed the others. When he returned home, the news informed him that it had indeed been a terrorist attack. He gloated momentarily at his validation, because he had been right.

After World War II, America became one of only two global super powers. Throughout the Cold War, not just Americans, but the entire world, lived under the very real threat of nuclear annihilation. With the fall of the Soviet Union, the world breathed a collective sigh of relief, then went right back to what they'd been doing. It took a while for anyone to even notice that now there was only one super power: the USA.

Without going into a long-winded synopsis of world history, the simple fact is that global super powers make enemies; it's almost impossible not to. The British Empire had some very powerful enemies. The Ottomans had enemies. The USSR had some very powerful enemies, and so on. Realistically, it's impossible to wield the power America does without becoming a target for radicals and power seekers around the world.

Americans only account for 5 percent of the world's population, yet we consume 26 percent of the world's energy. The only country that uses more energy than the United States, per capita, is Canada. For comparison, Italy consumes the least energy among the industrialized countries of the world. The US dollar is still the world's only reserve currency, as it has been since 1944. Since the fall of the Soviet Union, the United States is also the only military superpower. This is a fact that the United States and its allies have leveraged to get their way again and again in many international confrontations.

> Question: *"So with so many social and medical advancements we can bring to the independents, why would they fight so hard against us?"*
>
> Answer: *"We meddle. People don't like to be meddled with. We tell them what to do, what to think. Don't run, don't walk. We're in their homes and in their heads and we haven't the right. We're meddlesome."*
> -River Tam, *Serenity.* Movie, 2005.

Although the United States sits comfortably between peaceful Canada and impoverished Mexico, it's under constant threat of attack, not only from other governments, but also from international terrorist networks that are allowed to operate in these nations.

- North Korea. Experts estimate that North Korea has

about 1,000 ballistic missiles with advanced missile systems and nuclear weapons. There's still debate over whether or not North Korea has the technology to develop weapons that are capable of hitting targets within the continental US. However, North Korea openly attacked South Korea in 2010 with only the consequence of a stern lecture from the United Nations.

- Iran. With the help of China, Russia, and North Korea, Iran has greatly improved its missile systems and is currently working towards their own nuclear capability. There is much concern over the Shahab-class missiles they have, with a range of up to 2,000 km, but the real issue is the rumor that they are developing the Shahab-6, which would have a range up to 1,800 miles.

- Pakistan. Regardless of the spin, Pakistan is essentially a failed state. On top of the fact, it's a nuclear failed state. Pakistan's military leaders and its civilian government are openly antagonistic to one another, often pulling in opposite directions. The mountainous region between Pakistan and Afghanistan is a notorious "no man's land," from which various terrorist organizations base their operations. Then, of course, there's the fact that the world's most wanted man, Osama bin Laden, was hiding in Pakistan for years, right down the street from a major military installation.

- China. China has been stockpiling enough gold, rice, and

industrial metals to make anyone's eyebrow go up. They are a well-known nuclear power who has shown a willingness to sell ballistic weapons and technology to countries like North Korea and Iran. The United States will not move against China due to the fact that China is our largest creditor and holds the most US Treasuries. It is currently believed that China has approximately 200 nuclear-armed ballistic missiles, according to the Heritage Foundation.

Soft Targets

We have a long list of enemies and potential enemies, but the list of potential targets is even greater. US military bases are most vulnerable. The bases are, more often than not, guarded by unarmed or only lightly armed guards with wooden swing gates. This is not likely the best deterrent to any terrorist.

The goal of most terrorist groups is to create as much devastation as possible using the least resources possible. Thus, any "soft target," i.e., a lightly guarded building, factory, or military installation, is an ideal target for these groups. The following are a list of historical events that illustrate the damage a saboteur could inflict by exploiting a soft target:

In 1984, an accidental leak of toxic gas in India killed between 16,000-30,000 people and injured about 500,000. The toxic gas was methyl isocyanate, and in the United States it is manufactured extremely close to large urban cities. Why should a terrorist build and try to deploy a weapon here when the country already has these chemical plants in convenient locations for them?

Cleveland, Ohio saw a potential catastrophe in 1994 when a liquid natural gas (LNG) tank exploded and not only destroyed one square mile of the city, but burned 130 people alive. These tanks are everywhere thanks to the ever-increasing popularity of natural gas, and their locations are usually in facilities near densely populated cities. For the more traditional terrorist, there's the time-honored custom of blowing up your enemy's dams. Not only do you lose your water reserves but also the potential for death and suffering is enormous. In 2003, the American Society of Civil Engineers listed more than 10,000 dams in America as being "high hazard," meaning that there was a city less than 1 mile downstream.

The smallpox virus could have been eliminated long ago, but the United States and a few other countries just can't seem to let go of the potentially lethal weapon. The United States has spent over $20 billion on biodefense programs since 2001, and it's not just defense against smallpox. A number of laboratories across the nation work with dangerous pathogens such as: rift valley fever, Japanese encephalitis, foot and mouth disease, contagious bovine pleuropneumonia, and the nipah virus—which is only the tip of the iceberg. We fret that our enemy could release an epidemic on us, yet we grow them ourselves and place them in facilities within major population centers. Just one of those pathogens released into the population could cause a historic mega-disaster.

Targets for terrorist attacks are dangerously placed and have the potential for massive hardship on an enormous scale. Huge segments of the United States could be blacked out for a matter of days, or even months, if we suffered an attack on certain power grids. Inside substations are extremely hard to replace components that are crucial to our power supply. Hundreds of billions of dollars would be sucked from the economy as cascade failures, and these damaged components could theoretically take months to repair or replace. Depending on the season, the most vulnerable of the population could begin to die from hypothermia or hyperthermia.

For a long time, engineers and electric companies have known that the United States power grid has a severe vulnerability problem. The largest concern is the immense custom-built transformers, which increases the voltage of electricity to levels suitable for bulk transmission and then reduces the voltage for distribution to customers. The United States only manufactures a handful of these transformers. A cyber attack could demolish entire sections of the grid, if not the entire system. The Department of Homeland Security reported that the number of cyber attacks in 2012 increased by 52 percent and that of the 198 attacks reported during that year—82 of them were on the energy sector— several resulted in successful break-ins. Hurricanes like Sandy and Katrina have shown us that weather can bring down the grid for weeks.

Newt Gingrich authored a novel that portrays a nation of starved millions after unidentified enemies destroy the power grid via an electromagnetic pulse (EMP). A single nuclear weapon detonated in high-altitude, above 30 kilometers, would cause an EMP, and literally fry any electronics it reached. As of December 12th 2012, with the successful launch of an orbiting satellite, North Korea now has the potential to launch a devastating attack on America. Currently, North Korea is a mortal enemy of the US. Lt. General Ronald Burgess, the director of the Defense Intelligence Agency, testified to the Senate Armed Services Committee that North Korea has weaponized its nuclear devices into warheads for ballistic missiles. In the summer of 2004, a group of Russian generals warned the EMP Commission that secrets had been leaked to North Korea for a new nuclear weapon, a "super-EMP" (electromagnetic pulse) warhead. South Korean military intelligence has stated that Russian scientists are currently in North Korea helping to create this "super-EMP" device. Even a military adviser in China has said that North Korea does, in fact, have this weapon.

By estimates given by the Congressional EMP Commission, within one year of an EMP attack, two-thirds of the American population—roughly 200 million people—would be dead from starvation, disease, and societal collapse. Many speculate that North Korea and Iran are working together in this endeavor. The two countries could bring the entire world back into the Stone Age, or worse.

Chapter 7: When the Resources Stop Flowing

Three months after the collapse...

They had fought their way past the militia that had raided Monroe's home. They had made it to the truck and were now on the street. Mary, his son, and Monroe were uninjured. But James had taken a bullet through his upper arm and was clasping his hand as tightly as he could over the wound. "Mary, you'll need to find something to tie around James's arm," Monroe instructed, turning the truck down a road that headed off in the direction of the northern mountains. Mary did as instructed and tore off the bottom part of her pant leg, making a makeshift pressure bandage around her husband's arm.

James stared out the window of the truck absently surveying the landscape around them. They had been on the road for about an hour so far. Monroe said that he was surprised they had not hit any barricades, but he had taken the scenic mountain road for just that reason. In the distance, James saw billows of smoke rising from unknown buildings and wondered vaguely what had happened. It was odd to him; it had only been a few months since the US financial system had collapsed, and yet what he saw seemed to be from a scene out of a post-apocalyptic movie. He saw a few helicopters fly by in the distance, but they didn't look like any he had ever seen before. They had a whole different geometry to them and were bubble-shaped in the front. Not at all like the US helicopters, military or otherwise, he had seen before.

It wasn't long before they came upon the first "scene." James didn't know how to describe it. It was horrific, but he couldn't look away as they passed it. Dozens of bodies were piled several feet high, surrounded by signs saying "Down with America!" and "Fight the oppressors!" They drove on all the same; the dead didn't need help being dead. James did wonder who had killed them, though. "Where are we headed?" he asked Monroe.

"My brother's. It's not far." He gestured towards the mountain range to the north of them. "It's in that general direction."

Is the United States Military preparing for civil unrest here in America? In the Southern California desert the military constructed a mock city about the size of downtown San Diego, using about $170 million dollars of American tax dollars. It is one of the most sizable and most detailed training centers ever constructed. The Marine Corps states that the facility trains their forces to fight in urban environments, not unlike Kabul or Baghdad, but not unlike Los Angeles either. It consists of 1,560 buildings, 1,900 feet of underground tunnels, a man-made riverbed, dozens of courtyards, seven mock city districts, and spans 274 acres. More than 15,000 Marines can train simultaneously. Similar immersion training centers already exist. The military plans to open more at Marine Corps bases in North Carolina, Hawaii, and Okinawa.

Also, it bears repeating that America's police are militarizing rapidly. Thanks to the "War on Drugs" and the "War on Terror," the line between officer and soldier is blurring rapidly. In 1983, only 13 percent of towns with populations from 25,000-50,000 had SWAT teams. Now that number is up to 80 percent. The number of SWAT-style raids had skyrocketed as well. In 1983, there were 3,000 such raids in the US. By 2005, there were roughly 50,000. Has crime increased 1,667 percent since 1983? Or is there another reason for this massive domestic militarization? Perhaps America's leaders have seen the writing on the wall for some time. You don't have to be a rocket scientist to see that the nation's financial situation is worse than unsustainable; it's hopeless. Rioting and civil unrest are natural outcomes of a national default.

When the Pot Boils Over

In Greece, dockworkers blocked and protested ports in response to their current economic crisis and the strident terms of the country's bailouts. Riot police arrived and gave them an ultimatum, bringing their efforts to a stop: either go back to work or you're fired. However, workers from other sectors have walked away from their jobs in a show of support for the striking dockworkers. The situation in Greece is a window into the massive dysfunction of a bankrupt nation.

In Athens, large, violent groups overtook a protest against the bailout austerity measures in the city center. They hurled gasoline bombs into a bank, killing three workers. Anarchists in hoods and helmets, armed with bats and hammers, stormed the Parliament building, chanting "thieves, thieves." Protesters threw another gas bomb into Marfin Egnatia Bank, trapping over a dozen people—a man and two women died from smoke inhalation.

Already, factions are emerging as Greece's neo-Nazi party "Golden Dawn," also known as "Chrysi Avgi," have begun a public support drive in Germany. It says that its goal is to target Greeks who are moving to Germany to seek work. They have shown a willingness and readiness to use violence in Greece and may do so as well in Germany.

In Cyprus, citizens waited for days in endless lines outside Bank ATMs to withdraw cash needed for daily survival as merchants refused all credit cards for any transactions. As their banking crisis worsened, the government declared a one-time "tax" on all foreign account holders. Before the crisis, Cyprus had been a bit of an offshore tax haven for Russians. A bank holiday was declared, so it was impossible for anyone, citizen or not, to withdraw their money as the government confiscation took place. Always be leery when you hear of an unexpected "bank holiday."

Cypriots rocked back on their heels when they discovered that a company connected to the family of President Nicos Anastasiades moved their money out of one of the distressed banks just before the system went on lock down on March 15th. Reuters reported:

> Banks reopened last week but Cypriots can withdraw only 300 Euros ($390) a day under a range of controls imposed to prevent panicked residents from emptying their accounts or moving all their savings abroad. Hundreds of bank workers protested outside parliament on Thursday, worried that they could lose much of their pension savings under the terms of the bailout deal. This stipulates that some depositors have to bear part of the rescue's cost if their accounts hold more than 100,000 Euros ($128,500). "I am disappointed and angry," said Iacovos Louca, 53, who works at Popular Bank, which is being wound down under the $10 billion deal with the EU and International Monetary Fund. "The politicians are out of touch with our problems

> and the big guys, who had the information, managed to take their money abroad." A copy of a bank statement, first published in the Cypriot communist newspaper Haravgi, which maintains it is genuine, shows a company whose owners are related to the president by marriage moving money out of Popular in early March.

In Madrid, rioters and protesters clashed with police as the government canceled flights and shut down train service. One in four people are out of work in Spain. Factories have come to a standstill, and millions of workers are on strike. Riot police fired rubber bullets into the crowd of protesters and arrested several of them. In Rome, students stoned police and hurled bottles and firecrackers. The police responded with tear gas.

In Portugal, unemployment has jumped to a record 15.8 percent. Witnesses saw a Spanish woman jump to her death as bailiffs tried to evict her from her long time home. Protesters of Spain's austerity measures have jammed cash machines with glue and coins and stuck anti-government stickers on store windows.

With food prices, employment rates, and labor force participation plummeting, a new wound has been opened up to the public. IRS data has shown that during the economic downturn, the government gave out $80 million in unemployment benefits to American millionaire households, while targeting conservative groups that oppose unnecessary spending. The report reveals that about 3,200 households reporting an adjusted gross income of over $1 million collected unemployment, averaging $12,600 each, $29.9 million in total for 2010. Heidi Shierholz of the Economic Policy Institute claims that the benefits system is still "sound" and that 68 percent of the payments went to households that earned less than $50,000 a year.

It CAN Happen Here

In 1906, a devastating earthquake stuck San Francisco. That morning the mayor issued a proclamation that authorized law enforcement to "shoot to kill" any looters. The US Army eventually came in under the guise of "assistance." One man was bayoneted by a soldier after taking supplies with permission of the store's owner. Another man, who was attempting to rescue someone trapped in the rubble, was shot dead after being mistaken for a looter. No one knows how many departed from this world due to the actions of authorities. Estimates are as high as 500, but, apparently, the culprits threw the bodies into the flames and the bay, making it impossible to count them.

Of course, that was over a hundred years ago. That wouldn't happen today, would it? *Of course it would, and it has!* After Hurricane Katrina, officials took New Orleans police prematurely off of search and rescue duty and told them to protect property from looters. Officials told them they could shoot thieves, and police do not shoot to warn; they are taught to shoot to kill. The Glover story is a shocking glimpse into what authorities are capable of in a crisis. According to federal indictments, police officer David Warren shot Henry Glover for supposedly picking up stolen goods. Henry was a father of four. Henry's brother and a stranger took the injured man in their car to a nearby school. However, instead of providing medical care, the police reportedly beat the brother and stranger and torched the car, incinerating Henry, *still alive.*

Riots and a form of martial law have already taken place on American soil. In March 2013, the NYPD (New York Police Department) declared part of Brooklyn a "frozen zone," which has several parallels to marital law. This was in response to protests following the police shooting death of 16-year-old Kimani Gray. Two plain-clothed officers reportedly shot Gray seven times. On the Wednesday following the shooting, police arrested an estimated 46 people who had been protesting, including Gray's distraught sister. Again, riots led to looting at the Church Farm Market and a local Rite-Aid store.

Civil unrest is growing as groups of citizens come together in organizations such as the Occupy Movement, the Zeitgeist Movement, the Venus Project, and Anonymous. Born from the idea created during the Arab spring, the Occupy Movement states that they are the 99 percent. Their primary goal is to make the economic and political relations in all societies more equally distributed. Their first US protest was the well-publicized "Occupy Wall Street" in New York's Zuccotti Park. The protest began on September 17th, 2011. By October 9th, Occupy protests had taken place in over 95 cities across 82 countries. Authorities had removed most of the major camps by the end of 2011. Cornel West described the movement as a "democratic awakening."

The Zeitgeist Movement is a sustainability advocacy group. They promote their belief of a move from our traditional "monetary market" to a system based on the earth's resources. They state that the current socioeconomic system we have is structurally corrupt, and that people need to replace it with something more efficient. So far, they've produced three movies to promote their ideals.

The Venus Project is another group that advocates the elimination of the monetary system. Started by futurist Jacque Fresco, the project is one of the most ambitious groups. Their goal is to restructure society at the global level and change it into a resource-based economy. His ideas are based on sustainable cities, energy efficiency, natural resource management and advanced automation, with social cooperation and scientific methodology as its cornerstones.

Anonymous is a "hacktivist" group with no known leader. It came into existence in 2003 on the image board "4chan." The loosely associated group is strongly opposed to Internet censorship and surveillance. They have hacked several government websites, including a recent hack into North Korea's government site, in response to its leader's nuclear showplay. They have been dubbed: "digital Robin Hood," "Internet freedom fighters," and "anarchic cyber-guerrillas." The public can identify them by their stylized "Guy Fawkes" masks, made famous by the movie *V for Vendetta*.

Chapter 8 – The Boiling Point

While conducting a weather experiment in the 1960s, Edward Lorenz discovered that what happens on one side of the world dominoes into an effect on the other side of the world. He dubbed this "sensitive dependence on initial conditions" *The Butterfly Effect.*

On March 31, 2012, a factory explosion in Germany brought the substance PA-12 to the spotlight. The general public was not aware of this before, but it is an important component in car fuel lines. This catastrophe severely threatened the production of the entire automotive industry as the disaster cut the supply of PA-12 in half overnight. A factory fire in the United States, the Tohoku earthquake, and the tsunami in Japan, all caused a scarcity in specialized automotive parts. Car manufacturing suddenly hit a roadblock, inconveniencing consumers, causing already bankrupt car companies to bleed money, and putting thousands of automotive jobs at risk.

This is a perfect example of how vulnerable our overstressed systems are. A hiccup in the supply chain on the other side of the world is all it takes to throw our lives into chaos. Dr. Andrew Coburn, a researcher at the Centre for Risk Studies at Cambridge Judge Business School stated:

> It used to be the case that catastrophes on the other side of the world had little economic impact on the UK, but in today's interconnected world, few countries are isolated from the knock-on effects of catastrophes, whether it's a freeze in Europe, piracy around the Horn of Africa, or a pandemic in Asia.

If the protesting coffee farmers in Colombia were to go on strike, a very likely scenario given the current situation, prices would skyrocket around the world. Thousands of Americans would have to cut back on their coffee habits, since they no longer have the income to pay such high costs. Any coffee shop that didn't have the funds to weather the storm would close its doors and fire its employees. Hundreds of thousands of jobs would be lost. A ripple effect. All because of coffee protest in Colombia.

One of the largest and most advanced economies in the world, the Eurozone, is in the midst of a steep recession as many of its member nations teeter on the edge of default. David Korowicz, a physicist and systems ecologist, recently published a paper called, "Trade-Off: Financial System Supply-Chain Cross-Contagion: A Study in Global Systemic Collapse." Within it, he explains that within weeks of the next major economic shock, contagion would quickly spread through global supply chains and cause an irreversible global economic collapse. Korwicz states, "Neither wealth nor geography is a protection. Our evolved co-dependencies mean that we are all in this together."

As parts are manufactured and put together into larger, more complex parts of even more complex devices, the faster this interdependency develops. Each smart phone depends on dozens of parts that have no reasonable facsimile. If a factory were to go offline, the production of the entire device would grind to a halt.

In 2005, there were two billion connected devices. Five years later that number had tripled to six billion, and experts expect that by 2015, the number will be 16 billion. That means not only is our dependence on these devices and the systems that support them more critical, but the speed with which information now travels has reached unprecedented territory. The "flash crash" of the stock market in 2010 showed how quickly the turmoil can infect our highly interconnected systems.

Monetary Bubbles Bursting

> *If the American people ever allow private banks to control the issue of their currency, first by inflation, then by deflation, the banks and cor-*

> *porations that will grow up around them will deprive the people of all property until their children wake up homeless on the continent their Fathers conquered.* – Thomas Jefferson

The mindboggling situation the US government is in today is exactly what Thomas Jefferson and Andrew Jackson warned against, though I doubt they could have imagined that it would be this bad. Central banks around the world have printed money with reckless abandon and issued credit at an alarming rate for decades. What we are now experiencing is the proverbial "chickens coming home to roost."

This means that nearly all of the nations in the developed world are caught in a desperate situation that depends on issuing new bank debt just to keep servicing old debts. When the economy begins to contract, as is happening in Europe, the ability to service these old debts disappears and debtors become insolvent and default on these debts. Private banks follow the central bank's lead, issuing mountains of low-grade debt, leaving them extremely vulnerable to economic contractions.

The bailing out of insolvent banks, unfortunately, does not solve the problem. In fact, the risk of collapse is, more often than not, displaced or magnified over time, as can be seen in Spain. Their banks were floundering, so the country provided them bailouts, in turn increasing their national debt. This caused a huge concern over the financial health of their entire system, and Spanish bonds disappeared into the "just bailed out" banks. This led to those same banks becoming even more insolvent and then "pop!"— the bubble burst. Spain has been teetering on the edge between recession and depression for several years now.

David Korowicz postulates a more general scenario in his recent essay *Tipping Point: Near-Term Systemic Implications of a Peak in Global Oil Production*:

> As the economy contracts, then the customers of the utility have less to spend. A decline in revenue would mean that the utility income relative to the fixed costs would fall. If they want to maintain the network, they may have to raise the price of their service; this would drive away some customers, and cause others to use less services. Thus the utility revenue would fall further, requiring further price rises, spending falls and so on. If the utility cannot afford to maintain the network, the service deteriorates making it less attractive for customers, who drop out, reducing income and so on.

Worldwide, we currently have the most complex global economy in history. Let's consider a situation concerning our continued drought, and the cascade effect this might lead to.

- The drought destroys corn and wheat crops, causing food and energy prices to rise. Remember, we also use corn for ethanol, which the industry adds to our gasoline.

- Farmers beg the government for assistance, but with the federal debt and sequester, the government can provide little to no assistance.

- Citizens struggle to afford enough gas for their vehicles to get them to work so that they can buy the expensive food to feed their families.

- With gas prices so high, long-range food transportation becomes increasingly limited, and communities have to survive on resources that are relatively close to them.

- Looting takes hold as people begin to do whatever they can to get food for themselves, and billions of dollars in damages begin to rack up.

- Officials call in the police and military to cull the looting, which leads to riots and even more violence as people struggle to acquire supplies.

- The loss of purchasing power and commodity stocks throws the stock market into chaos.

- America begins its fall and supporting nations pull away so as not to be dragged down with it. Others try to push more money into the US's system to keep it afloat, all the while increasing their own debt and instability.

- Billions, who depend on America, both domestically and internationally, go hungry and die. Finger-pointing begins.

- Already high tensions lead to countries posturing and threatening to attack.

And again, here is how it plays out:

There was a windmill sitting upon the crest, and then a second and a third lined along the top of the slope, lazily spinning in the light wind. James sat up straighter then, his arm giving him a twinge from the sudden movement.

"Mary. Mary, wake up," he called to his wife who was slumbering in the backseat. "What is this?" he asked Monroe. "Our new home," he replied simply as they came to the top of the pass. A small cluster of a dozen or so houses came into view, and they descended down into the valley. "My brother owns that plot on the far north side."

The sun was just slipping into the horizon, and James noticed that several lights were coming on below. Street lamps mostly, but he saw no power lines coming into the modest town.

Suddenly, there were several men blocking their path down the slope, and Monroe brought the truck to a stop. The men outside approached the driver's side of the truck, and James saw that they were heavily armed. He reached for the gun that Monroe had given him earlier, but a shake of the other man's head told him to leave it under his seat.

"What's your business here?" one of the men asked.

"We're here to see Isaac Peirce. He's my brother." Another of the armed men turned away and looked to be speaking into some type of radio. James felt tense; when they had left, they had left with nothing, so they were out of ammo and not prepared for another fight.

The man on the radio nodded to the first. "Looks like you're good to go," he said and waved them to go ahead down the hill as the others slowly moved off the road to let them pass.

James released a breath he hadn't known he had been holding as they made their way into the town. He realized, now that they were closer, that more than street lamps flickered. Behind closed curtains, he recognized the telltale changing lights of television sets. The town was clean and seemed utterly peaceful. There were a few cars here and there, but for the most part, it looked as if bicycling was the most common mode of transportation. There was even a grocery store towards the center of town, and it didn't have any broken windows. James laughed.

"James?" questioned Mary. He couldn't help himself, he kept laughing. "Are you all right?"

He stopped a moment to catch his breath and wipe a tear from his eye. "It's like nothing happened..."

Chapter 9: Prepping Goes Mainstream: We All Need to be Prepared

It may seem a large jump to go from discussing the importance of coffee to the world economy, to the idea of emergency preparedness. However, my purpose in telling you a long story about coffee, about the current state of the economy, about real incidences of disasters and riots was to lead you to understand the urgent necessity of becoming prepared. If disaster struck tomorrow, what sort of situation would you and your family face?

Over the last few years, a new "movement" has been growing on the national stage, internationally even. It's hard to say what exactly sparked this new movement. Maybe it was watching the markets collapse in 2007, the failure of major European nations like Greece, or the numerous natural disasters that have been striking urban centers. Whatever the reason, millions of Americans have instinctively started preparing for emergencies.

Most of these people aren't building "bug-out vehicles" or installing a fallout shelters in the backyard, they're simply taking a few rational precautions to make sure they're not caught completely unaware if an emergency were to strike their area. Flashlights, batteries, and drinking water— these are the kinds of items that belong in any emergency preparedness kit. Strangely, members of the mainstream media seem to think that making an emergency preparedness plan is tantamount to wearing a tinfoil hat.

Clearly, it's easy to make fun of "paranoid preppers." We all know the stereotype: People living in bunkers, refuse to use technology, fear the government, etc. For years, we've been instructed by the media and the entertainment industry to look down on these people. These people live in constant "fear" motivated by "ignorance" and other sinister motives, or so the media claims.

For every one financial expert who tried to warn us about the housing bubble and the banking crisis, there were 100 others telling them they were just simple-minded and paranoid (there's that word again). So, who turned out to be right and who lost their shirt?

The point that I'm making here is simple: Most Americans, even the most reasonable ones, have been preprogrammed to ignore all warnings. Nobody wants to appear to be paranoid, do they?

Preparedness-minded Americans have always been stereotyped as rural, uneducated, dangerously paranoid, and mildly psychotic. In a very underhanded way, preppers have been lumped in with the likes of Ted Kaczynski, David Koresh, and even garden-variety tax evaders. But that's all beginning to change.

Modern Day Preppers

Ironically enough, now even the US government is extolling the virtues of storing drinking water, flashlights, canned food, etc. Have you seen FEMA's "you never know when the day before is the day before" ad campaign? It's quite an about-face from the ads cramming the feel-good ObamaCare platitudes down your throat. Frankly, I find it almost refreshing to see the government admit that it can't guarantee to fulfill your every need from cradle to grave, if only this once.

"Our research shows that people are not inclined to prepare because they believe an emergency won't happen in their community," said Peggy Conlon, president and CEO of the Ad Council. "In partnership with Secretary Napolitano, Administrator Fugate and the team at FEMA, these new insightful PSAs highlight the importance of year-round preparedness."

Although shows like *Doomsday Preppers* have, in many ways,

tried to drive the "prepper" stereotypes to the extreme for profit, they've actually done the opposite. Unintentionally, they've made the entire country more comfortable with the idea of preparing. They've also shown the TV watching population that not all preppers are shut-ins or whack-jobs.

There are some very clear signs that preparing is going "mainstream" in America. According to a National Geographic survey, more than 62 percent of Americans think the world will experience a major catastrophe in less than 20 years. It's estimated that 3 million Americans are now engaging in some level of emergency preparedness.

Preparedness Resources You Might Not Think Of

When most people think of emergence preparedness, their minds immediately go to elite military organizations like the Navy SEALs or Army Rangers. It's true these elite forces are trained to survive with little or no supplies in wilderness situations. However, the question you might ponder is whether or not that is the most relevant skill set you might need to protect your family in a major crisis scenario.

Chances are good that you won't be dropped from a helicopter into a remote forest with just the clothes on your back. You'd be a lot better off with a more practical preparedness plan that includes storing the right items and rehearsing your emergency evacuation procedures like lots of run-of-the-mill organizations do all the time.

For example, one interesting model of emergency preparedness is your local hospital. Because their work is too important to be interrupted by power outages, and because their services may be more needed in times of great crisis, hospitals invest heavily in preparedness. Hospitals have backup generators to ensure uninterrupted electricity. They have intense evacuation procedures and security lockdown plans. I bet you never thought of a hospital director as a prepper before.

Another often-overlooked emergency preparedness resource is the LDS Church. Mormons are encouraged to "prepare to be self-reliant in times of personal or widespread emergency." The church's website encourages members to keep a 3-month supply of food, drinking water, medication, and first-aid supplies. The basic LDS guidelines include communication devices and financial reserves. You might say that Mormons are the consummate preppers.

The Unprepared Are The Crazy Ones

Throughout this book, we've examined a host of situations that could suddenly boil over and interrupt our way of life. Some of these could cause irreparable damage. Yet there's still a stigma placed on those who are smart enough to take common-sense precautions. This is one of the first reality checks that new preppers go through. So take a moment to realize that you're not being irrational, paranoid, or crazy.

In almost every reasonable way, it's the unprepared who are crazy. Despite the fact that most of them believe, deep down, that a major catastrophic event will occur in their lifetimes, they refuse to prepare. They'd rather fit in and go along. Their mindset is that of a high school kid who's afraid of being made fun of. It's unfortunate, but it's also their choice, and their safety.

Local Disaster Preparedness

One of the first things you can do is to identify the most likely crisis events to occur in your local area and focus on those. Do you live in Tornado Alley? Do you live near a fault line? Is there a chance you could be snowbound by a massive blizzard? Do you live in a major city where widespread rioting is possible?

Use these scenarios as your motivation to make a plan and start gathering necessary items. Each of these scenarios will require a slightly different set of tools and supplies, although the anatomy of a crisis is also fairly predictable and patterned, but more on that in the next chapter.

Six months before the collapse...

"It really is a good idea," Mary said watching the news report. James nodded his head in lackadaisical agreement. He might have argued with her at one point in time, or made a backhanded quip about how a bunch of paranoid hoarders were trying to make their disease into a virtue. But he was too worn out.

It had been a tough day at the office, another tough day in a long string of tough days, in fact. It seemed like it had been going on for years, but it had been only a month and a half. With the stock market bouncing from euphoric gains to gut wrenching losses, no one seemed to know what to do. His suppliers were hesitant to give him quotes and all of his clients were afraid to place orders. All of his friends seemed to be in the same boat. Nobody knew what to make of the financial turmoil the nation was going through, except that it definitely wasn't good.

Of course, the news was running a sensationalist piece all about a local preparedness militia that was offering free training courses on emergency evacuations, home defense, and firearms. The man who'd done the interview with the skinny blonde news anchor actually seemed very rational and down to earth. He was a local EMT, and despite having a scruffy, mountain man beard, he gave the whole piece a lot of credibility. That's what Mary had really responded to.

"A lot of people ask me about building a reinforced shelter, then I ask them how long their food stockpile will last and

they haven't even got one," the man told the reporter with a smirk. "Just like anything else, emergency preparedness should start with the basics: food, water, candles, flashlights, batteries, and build on that foundation. The underground bunker can wait."

James had to hand it to him, the guy had a sense of humor. Mary had stayed quiet, listening intently to everything the man had said.

He was too tired to give the suggestions his full attention, but for the first time in his life, he felt like emergency preparedness did make a little sense. After all, now that he had a son he felt even more protective over his family. It couldn't hurt to be a little more safety-minded.

All in good time, he thought. James chuckled as he thought to himself that it was ironic that the he would procrastinate his family's emergency preparedness to watch his favorite show, set in a zombie apocalypse.

Chapter 10: Time for a Crisis Inventory

Yes, many of the financial, agricultural, and logistical systems we depend on everyday are teetering on the brink of collapse. Even a hiccup in the supply of something as seemingly humdrum as coffee could spark the instability and demonstrations that will push us over the edge. But if there's only one concept that I can get across, it's that there's no time to procrastinate. Just like FEMA says, you never know when the day before is the day before.

In the US, perhaps more than any other place on earth, we've been given the illusion that the nearest 7-Eleven will always be open, no matter what, that you can always go get what you need at Wal-Mart at the last minute. When your family's safety depends on it, don't wait until the last minute.

The simple truth is that, while the catastrophes are all unique, the ways in which humans react during a crisis are very predictable. One of the first reactions most people experience is, of course, denial. They underestimate the severity of the crisis, or the duration, and most assume that the local, state, and Federal Government will be there to help them. Remember that FEMA is the one running ads all about how to prepare your family for a crisis. It can take days for FEMA to mobilize in response to a sudden crisis. Don't count on FEMA.

The second stage of a major crisis situation is even more predictable than the first: Panic. Everyone's panic reaction is different, some people are overcome with fear, while others retreat into despair, and others grow violent. This is exactly why you need to be prepared in advance. You don't know how others will react in the wake of a crisis, but you can guarantee that they'll be capable of erratic behavior driven by intense stress.

The last place you want to be is at a grocery store filled with these stressed out folks, rushing around the store in a panic because all of the shelves are already picked clean. Here's the thing that most Americans don't realize: Supermarkets and grocery stores keep an average of three days worth of food in stock. That means during a crisis, the employees of the store alone could purchase the majority of the food staples available.

By the time the average customer arrives at the supermarket, the canned food aisle will be a wasteland. The bottled water will be scarce. This desperate situation repeats itself every time a major crisis strikes the US. Count on it.

I have spent months of my life talking to military and emergency preparedness experts and then compiling their knowledge into easy-to-follow lists that you can take to the store today. These lists make it easy to determine how much of each item to buy, based on the size of your family and the amount of time you choose to prepare for. I recommend preparing to provide everything your household needs for at least 72-hours.

I urge you to click on the link below to watch the video presentation about what you can do to make sure you're never in this situation. In this video, you will learn the three biggest mistakes most preppers make, and the two most important steps you can take right now to protect your family.

What's Your Plan B?

If you don't have an emergency preparedness plan, then your government has one for you: A FEMA camp. While you may be thinking of a nice summer camp, most of the FEMA camps I've seen and read about are more like a mixture of one part prison, two parts concentration camp, and two parts trailer park. If this doesn't sound like your cup of tea, just think of how miserable you would be before FEMA arrives. By the time FEMA rolls in with its tents and trailers, roughly 72-hours after the crisis event, you'll be starved for even the most basic creature comforts.

The point I'm making here is that waiting for FEMA is a one-way ticket to misery. Even if you do end up in a FEMA camp, which is no picnic, you'll likely have to endure days or even weeks of hardship before the camp is ready to take on refugees.

The most ideal solution is to create a series of backup systems that will sustain you, off-the-grid, for weeks. Of course, that type of planning and execution requires a serious investment in time and resources. At the very least, your family should have a 72-hour supply of food, water, shelter, and safety.

Fortune Favors the Prepared Mind

Don't think people in your area will riot or use violence? Think again. Just like our protagonist James, experiences in our fictional SHTF scenario, we would all be surprised by what our neighbors are capable of in a desperate situation. What would you do if your children were hungry?
How would you feel when your children look at you with sad eyes and ask, "Why didn't you plan for this?" That's just a glimpse into the emotions that would dominate many deci-

sions in a real crisis.

Could you do all this on your own without my guides? You bet. But for $7-$27, it is all laid out for you. Hours and months of research and real life preparing. If your time is worth more than $1 an hour, then this is a better deal. And you won't make all the common mistakes most people make.

Take the time to watch my videos and learn how to prepare your family as quickly and inexpensively as humanly possible. Because, in the words of FEMA's infamous radio ads, "You never know when the day before is the day before."

Bibliography

"US Debt Clock". Last Accessed 05 April 2013. http://www.usdebtclock.org

Kulshreshtha, S.N (1998). "A Global Outlook for Water Resources to the Year 2025". Water Resources Management 12 (3): 167–184.

DeNavas-Walt, Carmen, Bernadette D. , Proctor, and Jessica C. Smith, US Census Bureau, Current Population Reports, P60-239, Income, Poverty, and Health Insurance , Coverage in the United States: 2010

Talbot, John M. Grounds for Agreement: The Political Economy of the coffee Commodity Chain. Lanham: Rowman & Littlefield Publishers, Inc, 2004.

Goodman, David. "The International coffee Crisis: A Review of the Issues." In Confronting the coffee Crisis: Fair Trade, Sustainable Livelihood and Ecosystems in Mexico and Central America, edited by Christopher M. Bacon, Jonathan A. Fox, Stephen R. Gliessman,

Digum, Gregory and Nina Luttinger. The coffee Book: Anatomy of an Industry from Crop to the Last Drop. New York: The New Press, 1999.

Richard W. Niska, M.D., M.P.H. And Catharine W. Burt, Ed.D. "Bioterrorism and Mass Casualty Preparedness in Hospitals" Division of Health Care Statistics, 27 September 2005. Last Accessed 08 April 2013. http://www.cdc.gov/nchs/data/ad/ad364.pdf

Steven Chu, Secretary of Energy 2011. "US Department of Energy, Critical Materials Strategy". Energy.Gov. Last Accessed 05 April 2013. http://energy.gov/sites/

prod/files/DOE_CMS2011_FINAL_Full.pdf

Graeme Wearden "Eurozone crisis live: Protests and food handout shows Greek pain continues" The Guardian, 06 February 2013. Last Accessed 07 April 2013. http://www.guardian.co.uk/business/2013/feb/06/eurozone-crisis-spain-corruption-oecd-uk1

John Vidal "UN warns of looming worldwide food crisis in 2013" The Guardian, 13 October 2012. Last Accessed 07 April 2013. http://www.guardian.co.uk/global-development/2012/oct/14/un-global-food-crisis-warning

Suzanne Goldenberg "Drought that ravaged US crops likely to worsen in 2013, forecast warns" The Guardian, 21 March 2013. Last Accessed 07 April 2013. http://www.guardian.co.uk/environment/2013/mar/21/noaa-outlook-drought-worse-2013?INTCMP=ILCNETTXT3487

Dawn Kawamoto "Is coffee the New Leading Economic Indicator?" Daily Finance, August 11, 2011. http://www.dailyfinance.com/2011/08/11/is-coffee-the-new-leading-economic-indicator/http://www.dailyfinance.com/2011/08/11/is-coffee-the-new-leading-economic-indicator/http://www.dailyfinance.com/2011/08/11/is-coffee-the-new-leading-economic-indicator/

Lauren M Jacobson "Starbucks Case Study" Last accessed July 18, 2013 http://laurenmjacobson.wordpress.com/case-studies/starbucks-case-study/http://laurenmjacobson.wordpress.com/case-studies/starbucks-case-study/http://laurenmjacobson.wordpress.com/case-studies/starbucks-case-study/

Mortimer Zuckerman "A Jobless Recovery is a Phony Recovery" Wall Street Journal, Last Accessed July 20, http://online.wsj.com/article/SB100014241278873237

408045786014722619533366.html?mod=trending_now_1

Kenneth R. Wise “Global Population Growing Faster Than Expected” Los Angeles Times, July 10, 2013. http://www.latimes.com/news/science/sciencenow/la-sci-sn-global-population-growing-faster-than-thought-20130710,0,1785617.story

Radley Balko “Rise of the Warrior Cop” Wall Street Journal, July 22, 2013 http://online.wsj.com/article/SB10001424127887323848804578608040780519904.html

Nafeez Mosaddeq Ahmed “Why food riots are likely to become the new normal” The Guardian, 06 March 2013. Last Accessed 07 April 2013. http://www.guardian.co.uk/environment/blog/2013/mar/06/food-riots-new-normal

“NOAA predicts mixed bag of drought, flooding and warm weather for spring” NOAA, 21 March 2013. Last Accessed 08 April 2013. http://www.noaanews.noaa.gov/stories2013/20130321_springoutlook.html

Jeanne Bryner "Why the 1930s Dust Bowl Was So Bad." LiveScience, 04 May 2008. Last Accessed 05 April 2013. http://www.livescience.com/environment/080505-dust-bowl.html

Simmons “20 Deadliest Effects of Global Warming” Environmental Graffiti. Last Accessed April 09 2013. http://www.environmentalgraffiti.com/sciencetech/5-deadliest-effects-of-global-warming/

Jay K. “Top 10 Excuses People Use To Hate America” List Verse, 13 May 2009. Last Accessed 06 April 2013. http://listverse.com/2009/05/13/top-10-excuses-people-use-to-hate-america/

Cheesyweasel "10 Great Financial Collapses in History" List Verse, 10 August 2010. Last Accessed 06 April 2013. http://listverse.com/2010/08/10/10-great-financial-collapses-in-history/

Manny Fernandez "A Helium Shortage Leads to Fewer Balloons in the Sky" NY Times, 19 December 2012. Last Accessed 08 April 2013. http://www.nytimes.com/2012/12/20/us/a-helium-shortage-leads-to-fewer-balloons-in-the-sky.html

Matthew L. Wald "Terrorist Attack on Power Grid Could Cause Broad Hardship, Report Says" NY Times, 14 November 2012. Last Accessed 08 April 2013. http://www.nytimes.com/2012/11/15/science/earth/electric-industry-is-urged-to-gird-against-terrorist-attacks.html

Robert H. Frank "In the Real World of Work and Wages, Trickle-Down Theories Don't Hold Up" NY Times, 12 April 2007. Last Accessed 08 April 2013. http://www.nytimes.com/2007/04/12/business/12scene.html

Tamar Lewin "College May Become Unaffordable for Most in US" NY Times, 03 December 2008. Last Accessed 08 April 2013. http://www.nytimes.com/2008/12/03/education/03college.html

Al Baker "When the Police Go Military" NY Times, 03 December 2011. Last Accessed 08 April 2013. http://www.nytimes.com/2011/12/04/sunday-review/have-american-police-become-militarized.html

Dan Bilefsky "Three Reported Killed in Greek Protests" NY Times, 05 May 2010. Last Accessed 08 April 2013. http://www.nytimes.com/2010/05/06/world/europe/06greece.html

"China Stockpiling Rice, Iron Ore, Precious Metals and Dry Milk" Wealth Wire, 10 January 2013. Last Accessed 09 April 2013. http://www.wealthwire.com/news/global/4395

Reuters "Europe Austerity Protests: Strikes Sweep Southern Europe In Response To Cuts" Huffington Post, 14 November 2012. Last Accessed 05 April 2013. http://www.huffingtonpost.com/2012/11/14/europe-austerity-protests-strikes-greece-italy-france_n_2129091.html

Felicity A. Morse "Welfare Cuts Could Lead To 'Lord Of The Flies-Style Civil Unrest'" Huffington Post, 27 February 2013. Last Accessed 05 April 2013. http://www.huffingtonpost.co.uk/2013/02/27/welfare-cuts-lord-of-the-flies-civil-unrest-_n_2772706.html

"Cost of College Degree in U.S. Has Increased 1,120 Percent In 30 years, Report Says" Huffington Post, 15 August 2013. Last Accessed 05 April 2013. http://www.huffingtonpost.com/2012/08/15/cost-of-college-degree-increase-12-fold-1120-percent-bloomberg_n_1783700.html

Ryan J. Reilly "Eric Holder: Drone Strike To Kill U.S. Citizen On American Soil Legal, Hypothetically" Huffington Post, 05 February 2013. Last Accessed 06 April 2013. http://www.huffingtonpost.com/2013/03/05/us-drone-strike_n_2813857.html

Radley Balko "A Decade After 9/11, Police Departments Are Increasingly Militarized" Huffington Post, 12 September 2011. Last Accessed 06 April 2013. http://www.huffingtonpost.com/2011/09/12/police-militarization-9-11-september-11_n_955508.html

Radley Balko "ACLU Launches Nationwide Police Militarization Investigation" Huffington Post, 22 March 2013. Last Accessed 06 April 2013. http://www.huffingtonpost.com/2013/03/06/aclu-police-militarization-swat_n_2813334.html?1362577121

Radley Balko "Police 'Tank' Purchase Riles New Hampshire Town" Huffington Post, 16 February 2012. Last Accessed 06 April 2013. http://www.huffingtonpost.com/2012/02/16/police-tank-purchase-new-hampshire_n_1279983.html

"Despite progress, food insecurity remains pressing challenge" United Nations, 04 April 2013. Last Accessed 05 April 2013.
http://www.un.org/apps/news/story.asp?NewsID=44560&Cr=Food+security&Cr1=#.UWG3WVdc04o

"Deputy UN chief calls for urgent action to tackle global sanitation crisis" United Nations, 21 March 2003. Last Accessed 05 April 2013. http://www.un.org/apps/news/story.asp?NewsID=44452&Cr=sanitation&Cr1=#.UVOS2Fdc3Qq

"National Report on Efforts to Mitigate Desertification in the Western United States." United Nations Convention to Combat Desertification (UNCCD). 2006. Last Accessed 05 April 2013. http://www.unccd.int/cop/reports/otheraffected/national/2006/united_states_of_america-eng.pdf

"Water Cooperation – Facts and Figures" United Nations – Water, 2013. Last Accessed 05 April 2013. http://www.unwater.org/water-cooperation-2013/water-cooperation/facts-and-figures/en/

"Millions lack safe water" United Nations – Water, 2013. Last Accessed 05 April 2013. http://water.org/water-crisis/water-facts/water/

Julie Watson "$170 million mock city rises at Marine base" Associated Press, 26 January 2011. Last Accessed 08 April 2013. http://www.nbcnews.com/id/41258569/ns/us_news-life/t/million-mock-city-rises-marine-base/#.UWGnzldc04phttp://www.nbcnews.com/id/41258569/ns/us_news-life/t/million-mock-city-rises-marine-base/#.UWGnzldc04phttp://www.nbcnews.com/id/41258569/ns/us_news-life/t/million-mock-city-rises-marine-base/#.UWGnzldc04p

Press Release "Press Release FEMA and the Ad Council Unveil New Series of Ready PSAs as Part of Ninth Annual National Preparedness Month" September 13, 2012. http://www.adcouncil.org/News-Events/Press-Releases/FEMA-and-the-Ad-Council-Unveil-New-Series-of-Ready-PSAs-as-Part-of-Ninth-Annual-National-Preparedness-Monthhttp://www.adcouncil.org/News-Events/Press-Releases/FEMA-and-the-Ad-Council-Unveil-New-Series-of-Ready-PSAs-as-Part-of-Ninth-Annual-National-Preparedness-Monthhttp://www.adcouncil.org/News-Events/Press-Releases/FEMA-and-the-Ad-Council-Unveil-New-Series-of-Ready-PSAs-as-Part-of-Ninth-Annual-National-Preparedness-Month

Meg Gleason "The Results Are In: Is It The End Of The World As We Know it? Survey Says!" National Geographic, February 7, 2012. http://tvblogs.nationalgeographic.com/2012/02/07/the-results-are-in-is-it-the-end-of-the-world-as-we-know-it-survey-says/

Cindy Perman "Argggh! American workers are at a breaking point" CNBC, 09 April 2013. Last Accessed 09 April 2013. http://www.nbcnews.com/business/argggh-american-workers-are-breaking-point-1C9275554

Peter Vincent Pry "PRY: North Korea EMP attack could destroy U.S. — now" The Washington Times, 19 December 2012. Last Accessed 10 April 2013. http://www.washingtontimes.com/news/2012/dec/19/north-korea-emp-attack-could-destroy-us-now/

Grady Means "U.S. economy on schedule to crash March 2014 , America's fall will take global economies with it" The Washington Times, 25 October 2012. Last Accessed 10 April 2013. http://www.washingtontimes.com/news/2012/oct/25/us-economy-on-schedule-to-crash-march-2014/

Mattea Kramer "You ask, We answer: How Much Does the U.S. Spend on Foreign Aid" National Priorities, 22 October 2012. Last Accessed 07 April 2013. http://nationalpriorities.org/blog/2012/10/22/you-ask-we-answer-how-much-does-us-spend-foreign-aid/

"President Obama's Fiscal Year 2013 Budget" National Priorities 29 March 2012. Last Accessed 07 April 2013. http://nationalpriorities.org/en/analysis/2012/presidents-budget-fy2013/education/

Mary Kay Henry, Christine L. Owens "Hardworking Americans should not be living in poverty" CNN, 25 July 2012. Last Accessed 08 April 2013. http://www.cnn.com/2012/07/25/opinion/henry-owens-minimum-wage

William J. Bennett "The looming crisis of student loan debt" CNN, 06 December 2013. Last Accessed 08 April 2013.
http://www.cnn.com/2012/12/06/opinion/bennett-student-debt

Madison Park "Where in the world can you get universal health care?" CNN, 29 June 2012. Last Accessed 08 April 2013.
http://www.cnn.com/2012/06/28/health/countries-health-care

David Goldman "Hacker hits on U.S. power and nuclear targets spiked in

2012" CNN, 09 January 2013. Last Accessed 08 April 2013. http://money.cnn.com/2013/01/09/technology/security/infrastructure-cyberattacks/index.html

Parija Kavilanz "Doctors looking for an out" CNN, 10 January 2013. Last Accessed 08 April 2013.
http://money.cnn.com/gallery/smallbusiness/2013/01/09/doctors-quitting-reasons/index.html

Aaron Smith "Cash Strapped Farmers Feed Candy to Cows" CNN, 10 October 2012. Last Accessed 08 April 2013.
http://money.cnn.com/2012/10/10/news/economy/farmers-cows-candy-feed/index.html

Luke Landes "Resist Planned Obsolescence or Accept the Financial Consequences" Forbes, 06 November 2012. Last Accessed 06 April 2013.
http://www.forbes.com/sites/moneybuilder/2012/11/06/resist-planned-obsolescence-or-accept-the-financial-consequences/

Stuart Anderson "Doctor, Doctor, Why Won't America Let In More Doctors?" Forbes, 02 December 2012. Last Accessed 08 April 2013.
http://www.forbes.com/sites/stuartanderson/2012/12/02/doctor-doctor-why-wont-america-let-in-more-doctors/

Charles Kadlec "The Federal Reserve's Explicit Goal: Devalue the Dollar 33%" Forbes, 06 February 2012. Last Accessed 08 April 2013.
http://www.forbes.com/sites/charleskadlec/2012/02/06/the-federal-reserves-explicit-goal-devalue-the-dollar-33/

Jason Kane "Health Costs: How the U.S. Compares With Other Countries" PBS,

22 October 2012. Last Accessed 07 April 2013. http://www.pbs.org/newshour/rundown/2012/10/health-costs-how-the-us-compares-with-other-countries.html

"The War that made America" PBS, 18 January 2013. Last Accessed 07 April 2013. http://www.pbs.org/thewarthatmadeamerica/

"U.S. Federal Budget Analysis" US Government Spending, 2013. Last Accessed 05 April 2013. http://www.usgovernmentspending.com/federal_budget_detail_fy13bs12012n_20252421_501_502#usgs302

Chris Warren "10 Popular Jobs to Outsource" How Stuff Works, 30 September 2011. Last Accessed 09 April 2013.
http://www.howstuffworks.com/10-jobs-to-outsource.htm

Roger J. Moncarz, Michael G. Wolf, Benjamin Wright "Service-providing occupations, offshoring, and the labor market" US Bureau of Labor Statistics, December 2008. Last Accessed 08 April 2013. http://www.bls.gov/opub/mlr/2008/12/art4full.pdf

Bob Flach ""Livestock and Products Semi-annual – Supply tightens, prices surge" USDA Foreign Agricultural Service, 26 February 2013. Last Accessed 07 April 2013. http://gain.fas.usda.gov/Recent%20GAIN%20Publications/Livestock%20and%20Products%20Semi-annual_The%20Hague_EU-27_2-26-2013.pdf

Natalya Sinitsa "coffee Crisis in Full Swing in Colombia" Pravada, 03 April 2013. Last Accessed 04 April 2013. http://english.pravda.ru/business/companies/04-03-2013/123952-coffee_colombia-0/

"Which countries can deliver a tactical nuclear attack? Who might be able to do so in the near future?" Intellectual Take-Out. Last Accessed 08 April 2013. http://www.intellectualtakeout.org/faq/7-which-countries-can-deliver-tactical-nuclear-attack-who-might-be-able-do-so-near-future

"The Organisation for Economic Co-operation and Development" OECD. Last Accessed 08 April 2013. http://www.oecd.org/about/

"Riots & Violence to follow as Anger Erupts in Cyprus – Salt on Wounds" Commodity Trade Mantra, 06 April 2013. Last Accessed 07 April 2013. http://www.commoditytrademantra.com/eurozone/riots-violence-to-follow-as-anger-erupts-in-cyprus-salt-on-wounds/

Robert Kennedy "Food riots predicted over US crop failure" Aljazeera, 21 August 2012. Last Accessed 08 April 2013. http://www.aljazeera.com/indepth/features/2012/08/20128218556871733.html

Dan Goldberg "Health care costs rise far faster than wages; squeezing middle-class families" The Star Ledger, 13 December 2013. Last Accessed 07 April 2013. http://www.nj.com/news/index.ssf/2012/12/health_care_costs_rise_far_fas.html

Yves Smith "Student Loan Bubble So Big It's Trumping Credit Cards as a Spending Driver" Naked Capitalism, 04 March 2013. Last Accessed 06 April 2013. http://www.nakedcapitalism.com/2013/03/student-loan-bubble-so-big-its-trumping-credit-cards-as-a-spending-driver.html

"Medicare Begins Latest Pay-For-Performance Effort; Hospital Readmissions Among Program Targets" Kaiser Health News, 01 October 2013. Last Accessed

08 April 2013. http://www.kaiserhealthnews.org/Daily-Reports/2012/October/01/medicare-pay-for-performance.aspx

Mary Ellen Schneider "Readmission Rates Still Poor, Vary by Region" Hospitalist News, 06 February 2013. Last Accessed 08 April 2013.
http://www.ehospitalistnews.com/news/perioperative-medicine/single-article/readmission-rates-still-poor-vary-by-region/2ac046bb2ec64b8fd108aa2e-9730a5b7.html

Larry Bradley "The Butterfly Effect" Space Telescope Science Institute, 2010. Last Accessed 08 April 2013.
http://www.stsci.edu/~lbradley/seminar/butterfly.html

Andrew Coburn "Crash, crisis, calamity: system shock in a globalised world" University of Cambridge, 01 October 2012. Last Accessed 08 April 2013.
http://www.cam.ac.uk/research/news/crash-crisis-calamity-system-shock-in-a-globalised-world

Matthew Boesler "Citi Presents 14 Global Hot Spots That Have The Potential To Explode" Business Insider, 06 August 2012. Last Accessed 08 April 2013.
http://www.businessinsider.com/citi-geopolitical-risks-2012-8

Matthew Boesler "Expert Explains In Detail How The Next Shock Will Shatter The Global Economy" Business Insider, 07 August 2012. Last Accessed 08 April 2013. http://www.businessinsider.com/trade-off-financial-system-supply-chain-cross-contagion-a-study-in-global-systemic-collapse-2012-8?op=1

David Korowicz "Trade-Off , Financial System Supply-Chain Cross-Contagion: a study in global systemic collapse" Metris Risk Consulting & Feasta, 30

June 2012. Last Accessed 08 April 2013. http://www.feasta.org/wp-content/uploads/2012/06/Trade-Off1.pdf

"Pediatric Shortages, Long Wait Times Reinforce Need for Improved Access to Health Care for Children" PR Newswire, 23 July 2012. Last Accessed 07 April 2013.
http://www.prnewswire.com/news-releases/pediatric-shortages-long-wait-times-reinforce-need-for-improved-access-to-health-care-for-children-163386956.html

Tom Philpott "Canada says no to ethanol waste as cow feed, and more" Grist, 27 March 2008. Last Accessed 08 April 2013.
http://grist.org/article/meat-wagon-waste-makes-haste/

Ambrose Evans-Pritchard "China Warns Federal Reserve Over 'Printing Money'" The Telegraph, 24 May 2009. Last Accessed 07 April 2013.
http://www.telegraph.co.uk/finance/financialcrisis/5379285/China-warns-Federal-Reserve-over-printing-money.html

Harriet Alexander "Former Prime Minister Geir Haarde of Iceland says he did not cause financial chaos" The Telegraph, 28 April 2012. Last Accessed 07 April 2013.
http://www.telegraph.co.uk/news/worldnews/europe/iceland/9233418/Former-prime-minister-Geir-Haarde-of-Iceland-says-he-did-not-cause-financial-chaos.html

Fred Pearce "From ocean to ozone: Earth's nine life-support systems" New Scientist, 2010. Last Accessed 07 April 2013.
http://www.newscientist.com/special/ocean-to-ozone-earths-nine-life-support-

systems

"Dehydration – A Major Health Concern" Water Industry News. Last Accessed 05 April 2013.
http://www.waterindustry.org/Water-Facts/dehydration-1.htm

David Gutierrez "Natural Disasters Up More Than 400 Percent in Two Decades" Natural News, 05 June 2008. Last Accessed 06 April 2013.
http://www.naturalnews.com/023362_natural_disasters_floods.html

"Natural Disasters Hitting More People, Becoming More Costly" International Monetary Fund, 10 October 2012. Last Accessed 07 April 2013.
http://www.imf.org/external/pubs/ft/survey/so/2012/new101012a.htm

"The 10 Worst Disaster of the Last Century" Popular Mechanics, 2007. Last Accessed 07 April 2013.
http://www.popularmechanics.com/outdoors/survival/stories/10-disasters

"H.R. 6566 (112th): Mass Fatality Planning and Religious Considerations Act" Govtrack.us, 28 September 2012. Last Accessed 07 April 2013.
http://www.govtrack.us/congress/bills/112/hr6566/text

"H.R. 6715 (112th): To authorize the Secretary of Homeland Security, acting through the Administrator of the Federal Emergency Management Agency..." Govtrack.us, 27 December 2012. Last Accessed 07 April 2013. http://www.govtrack.us/congress/bills/112/hr6715/text

Permanent Subcommittee on Investigations "Federal Support for and Involvement in State and Local Fusion Centers" United States Senate, 03 October 2012.

Last Accessed 07 April 2013.

http://cdn.govexec.com/media/gbc/docs/pdfs_edit/100312cc1.pdf

"The Debt to the Penny and Who Holds It" Treasury Direct, 2013. Last Accessed 08 April 2013.

http://www.treasurydirect.gov/NP/BPDLogin?application=np

Stan Reybern "10 Governments That Went Bankrupt" Bill Shrink, 29 December 2009. Last Accessed 06 April 2013.

http://www.billshrink.com/blog/6799/10-governments-that-went-bankrupt/

'Mike' "Dollar Devaluation since 1913" Compare gold and Silver Prices, 23 January 2013. Last Accessed 06 April 2013.

http://www.comparegoldandsilverprices.com/dollar-devaluation-since-1913/

Andrew Taylor "Senate Democrats Pass $1 Trillion in New Taxes" Associated Press, 23 February 2013. Last Accessed 06 April 2013.

http://dailycaller.com/2013/03/23/senate-democrats-pass-1-trillion-in-new-taxes/

"Global Aging 2013: Rising to the Challenge" Standards and Poors, 20 March 2013. Last Accessed 07 April 2013.

http://www.standardandpoors.com/ratings/articles/en/us/?articleType=HTML&assetID=1245349076851

Valentina Pop "Cyprus becomes fifth eurozone country to seek bailout" EU observer, 26 June 2012. Last Accessed 06 April 2013. http://euobserver.com/economic/116753

Andrew Becker "Local Cops Ready for War With Homeland Security-Funded Military Weapons" The Daily Beast, 21 December 2011. Last Accessed 08 April 2013.
http://www.thedailybeast.com/articles/2011/12/20/local-cops-ready-for-war-with-homeland-security-funded-military-weapons.html

"The Militarization of Policing America" ACLU, 2013. Last Accessed 09 April 2013.
http://www.aclu.org/militarization

eVenues "A Brief History of coffee Houses as Meeting Places" eVenues, 07 February 2012. Last Accessed 06 April 2013.
http://blog.evenues.com/post/2012/02/07/A-Brief-History-Of-coffee-Houses-as-Meeting-Places.aspx

Rob Waugh "Rising populations driving Earth towards a disastrous 'tipping point' where humanity starves itself out" The Daily Mail, 06 June 2012. Last Accessed 08 April 2013.
http://www.dailymail.co.uk/sciencetech/article-2155322/Rising-populations-driving-Earth-irreversible-tipping-point--scientists-global-government.html7

Clara Piccirillo, PhD "Future Element Shortage: the Problems and the Challenges of Running Low" Decoded Science, 29 January 2013. Last Accessed 08 April 2013.
http://www.decodedscience.com/element-shortage-phosphorus-dysprosium/24539

"North Korean EMP attack could destroy U.S.A." Veterans Today, 11 January

2013. Last Accessed 08 April 2013.
http://www.veteranstoday.com/2013/01/11/north-korean-emp-attack-could-destroy-u-s-a/

Roberton Williams "The Numbers: What are the Federal Government's sources of revenue" Urban Institute and Brookings Institution, 13 September 2011. Last Accessed 06 April 2013.
http://www.taxpolicycenter.org/briefing-book/background/numbers/revenue.cfm

Stefanie Spencer "The coffee House – A History" INeedcoffee, May 2009. Last Accessed 07 April 2013.
http://www.ineedcoffee.com/09/london-coffee-house/

Peter Turchin "Social Tipping Points and Trend Reversals: A Historical Approach" University of Connecticut, May 2011. Last Accessed 05 April 2013.
http://cliodynamics.info/PDF/TrendReversal.pdf

'Michael' "10 Tipping Points Which Could Potentially Plunge The World Into A Horrific Economic Nightmare" The Economic Collapse Blog, 07 June 2011. Last Accessed 07 April 2013.
http://theeconomiccollapseblog.com/archives/10-tipping-points-which-could-potentially-plunge-the-world-into-a-horrific-economic-nightmare

Robert Wilde "The Crisis of the 1780's and the Causes of the French Revolution" About.com. Last Accessed 06 April 2013.
http://europeanhistory.about.com/od/thefrenchrevolution/a/hfr2.htm

Mark Strauss "Looking Back on the Limits of Growth", Smithsonian magazine,

April 2012. Last Accessed 07 April 2013.
http://www.smithsonianmag.com/science-nature/Looking-Back-on-the-Limits-of-Growth.html

"Ending the Depression Through Planned Obsolescence" Bernard London, 1932. Last Accessed 05 April 2013.
http://upload.wikimedia.org/wikipedia/commons/2/27/London_%281932%29_Ending_the_depression_through_planned_obsolescence.pdf

Wallace "Impact of the coffee Crisis" Catie. Last Accessed 03 April 2013.
http://web.catie.ac.cr/eventos/conferencias/Memoria_Wallace2/Fullpaper/Ted%20Lingle%20full%20paper.pdf

"Calling it quits: Labor force participation rate hits 34-year low in US" Russia Today, 05 April 2013. Last Accessed 05 April 2013.
http://rt.com/usa/rate-jobs-americans-labor-405/

"Recession saw US millionaires claim millions in unemployment" Russia Today, 06 April 2013. Last Accessed 07 April 2013.
http://rt.com/usa/benefits-million-households-unemployment-423/

Rebecca Solnit "Looters and the lessons of Katrina" LA Times, 29 August 2010. Last Accessed 06 April 2013.
http://articles.latimes.com/2010/aug/29/opinion/la-oe-solnit-katrina-looting-20100829

Abby Ellin "Looters Arrested in Post-Superstorm Spree" ABC News, 02 November 2012. Last Accessed 06 April 2013.

http://abcnews.go.com/blogs/business/2012/11/looters-arrested-in-post-super-storm-spree/

Cara Batema "Colombian coffee farmers rioting" Examiner, 26 February 2013. Last Accessed 05 April 2013.
http://www.examiner.com/article/colombian-coffee-farmers-rioting

Herb Weisbaum "Interest on government student loans set to double this summer" Today, 09 April 2013. Last Accessed 09 April 2013.
http://lifeinc.today.com/_news/2013/04/09/17666719-interest-on-government-student-loans-set-to-double-this-summer?lite

"coffee Shop Business Report" SBDC Net, 2012. Last Accessed 09 April 2013.
http://www.sbdcnet.org/small-business-research-reports/coffee-shop-2012

Charles W. Bryant "How long can you go without food and water?"How Stuff Works, 11 February 2008. Last Accessed 08 April 2013.
http://adventure.howstuffworks.com/survival/wilderness/live-without-food-and-water1.htm

Trent Stockton "Caffeine withdrawal study" Johns Hopkins Medicine, 29 September 2004. Last Accessed 07 April 2013.
http://www.hopkinsmedicine.org/press_releases/2004/09_29_04.html

Nestor Osorio "The Global coffee Crisis: A Threat to Sustainable Development" ICO, 21 August 2002. Last Accessed 06 April 2013.
http://dev.ico.org/documents/globalcrisise.pdf

Alex Kingsbury "6 Vulnerable Potential Terrorist Targets" US News. Last Ac-

cessed 06 April 2013.
http://www.usnews.com/news/slideshows/six-vulnerable-potential-terrorist-targets/

Steven Nelson "Kimani Gray Shooting Death Prompts Looting, Rioting in Brooklyn" US News, 14 March 2013. Last Accessed 06 April 2013.
http://www.usnews.com/news/newsgram/articles/2013/03/14/kimani-gray-shooting-death-prompts-looting-rioting-in-brooklyn

Matt Ferner, "The 1,000 Year Storm: Colorado's Flood Is One For The History Books." Accessed 10 October 2013
http://www.huffingtonpost.com/2013/09/20/1000-year-storm_n_3956897.html

Dale Collette, "Who, What, Why: How long can someone survive without food?" Accessed 10 October, 2013 http://www.bbc.co.uk/news/magazine-17095605
"Discussion: The Physiology and Treatment of Starvation" Accessed 09 August, 2013 http://www.ncbi.nlm.nih.gov/pmc/articles/PMC2181967/

Jeffrey Magers, "Hollow point ammunition is more effective and safer to use." Accessed 07 August, 2013. www.homelandsecuritynewswire.com/dr20130506-hollow-point-ammunition-is-more-effective-and-safer-to-use

Rob Jordan, "Is A Global Tipping Point Approaching?" Accessed 08 August, 2013 http://woods.stanford.edu/news-events/news/global-tipping-point-approaching
Water Filter Program, Acceessed 29 July, 2013. http://www.bootsontheground.org/water-filter-program/

David Korwitz, "Tipping Point: Near-Term Systemic Implications of a Peak in Global Oil Production - An Outline Review" Accessed 29 July, 2013. http://

www.feasta.org/2010/03/15/tipping-point-near-term-systemic-implications-of-a-peak-in-global-oil-production-an-outline-review/

Made in the USA
Monee, IL
04 November 2026

67381723R10079